HIV/AIDS

Other Books of Related Interest:

At Issue Series
H1N1 Flu
Transgendered People

Current Controversies Series
Health Care

Global Viewpoints Series
Death and Dying
Discrimination
Homosexuality
Human Rights

Introducing Issues with Opposing Viewpoints Series
AIDS
Gay Marriage
Vaccines

Opposing Viewpoints Series
The Catholic Church
Epidemics
Gays in the Military
Sexually Transmitted Diseases

GLOBAL VIEWPOINTS

HIV/AIDS

Noah Berlatsky, Book Editor

GREENHAVEN PRESS
A part of Gale, Cengage Learning

GALE
CENGAGE Learning

Detroit • New York • San Francisco • New Haven, Conn • Waterville, Maine • London

Elizabeth Des Chenes, *Managing Editor*

© 2012 Greenhaven Press, a part of Gale, Cengage Learning

Gale and Greenhaven Press are registered trademarks used herein under license.

For more information, contact:
Greenhaven Press
27500 Drake Rd.
Farmington Hills, MI 48331-3535
Or you can visit our Internet site at gale.cengage.com

For product information and technology assistance, contact us at

Gale Customer Support, 1-800-877-4253
For permission to use material from this text or product, submit all requests online at
www.cengage.com/permissions

Further permissions questions can be emailed to permissionrequest@cengage.com

Articles in Greenhaven Press anthologies are often edited for length to meet page requirements. In addition, original titles of these works are changed to clearly present the main thesis and to explicitly indicate the author's opinion. Every effort is made to ensure that Greenhaven Press accurately reflects the original intent of the authors. Every effort has been made to trace the owners of copyrighted material.

Cover image © Gideon Mendel/Corbis.

LIBRARY OF CONGRESS CATALOGING-IN-PUBLICATION DATA

HIV/AIDS / Noah Berlatsky, book editor.
    p. cm. -- (Global viewpoints)
    Summary: "HIV/AIDS: The Spread of the HIV/AIDS Epidemic; Treatment of HIV/
  AIDS; Moral Issues and HIV/AIDS; Discrimination and HIV/AIDS" -- Provided by
  publisher.
    Includes bibliographical references and index.
    ISBN 978-0-7377-5656-2 (hardback) -- ISBN 978-0-7377-5657-9 (pbk.)
    1. HIV infections--Juvenile literature. 2. AIDS (Disease)--Juvenile literature. I.
Berlatsky, Noah.
    RA643.8.H54 2011
    614.5'99392--dc22

                                                         2011008699

Printed in the United States of America
1 2 3 4 5 6 7 15 14 13 12 11

Contents

Chapter 1: The Spread of the HIV/AIDS Epidemic

Senegal has had substantial success in fighting HIV/AIDS. Its aggressive government response to the epidemic included promotion of condom use, educational efforts, and the involvement of religious and community leaders.

Chapter 2: Treatment of HIV/AIDS

Chapter 3: Moral Issues and HIV/AIDS

Chapter 4: Discrimination and HIV/AIDS

Foreword

> "The problems of all of humanity can
> only be solved by all of humanity."
> —Swiss author Friedrich Dürrenmatt

Global interdependence has become an undeniable reality. Mass media and technology have increased worldwide access to information and created a society of global citizens. Understanding and navigating this global community is a challenge, requiring a high degree of information literacy and a new level of learning sophistication.

Building on the success of its flagship series, *Opposing Viewpoints*, Greenhaven Press has created the *Global Viewpoints* series to examine a broad range of current, often controversial topics of worldwide importance from a variety of international perspectives. Providing students and other readers with the information they need to explore global connections and think critically about worldwide implications, each *Global Viewpoints* volume offers a panoramic view of a topic of widespread significance.

Drugs, famine, immigration—a broad, international treatment is essential to do justice to social, environmental, health, and political issues such as these. Junior high, high school, and early college students, as well as general readers, can all use *Global Viewpoints* anthologies to discern the complexities relating to each issue. Readers will be able to examine unique national perspectives while, at the same time, appreciating the interconnectedness that global priorities bring to all nations and cultures.

Material in each volume is selected from a diverse range of sources, including journals, magazines, newspapers, nonfiction books, speeches, government documents, pamphlets, organization newsletters, and position papers. *Global Viewpoints* is truly global, with material drawn primarily from international sources available in English and secondarily from US sources with extensive international coverage.

Features of each volume in the *Global Viewpoints* series include:

- An **annotated table of contents** that provides a brief summary of each essay in the volume, including the name of the country or area covered in the essay.

- An **introduction** specific to the volume topic.

- A **world map** to help readers locate the countries or areas covered in the essays.

- For each viewpoint, an **introduction** that contains notes about the author and source of the viewpoint explains why material from the specific country is being presented, summarizes the main points of the viewpoint, and offers three **guided reading questions** to aid in understanding and comprehension.

- **For further discussion** questions that promote critical thinking by asking the reader to compare and contrast aspects of the viewpoints or draw conclusions about perspectives and arguments.

- A worldwide list of **organizations to contact** for readers seeking additional information.

- A **periodical bibliography** for each chapter and a **bibliography of books** on the volume topic to aid in further research.

- A comprehensive **subject index** to offer access to people, places, events, and subjects cited in the text, with the countries covered in the viewpoints highlighted.

Global Viewpoints is designed for a broad spectrum of readers who want to learn more about current events, history, political science, government, international relations, economics, environmental science, world cultures, and sociology—students doing research for class assignments or debates, teachers and faculty seeking to supplement course materials, and others wanting to understand current issues better. By presenting how people in various countries perceive the root causes, current consequences, and proposed solutions to worldwide challenges, *Global Viewpoints* volumes offer readers opportunities to enhance their global awareness and their knowledge of cultures worldwide.

Introduction

"We are sending a clear message that breastfeeding is a good option for every baby, even those with HIV-positive mothers, when they have access to ARVs [antiretroviral drugs]."

—Daisy Mafubelu,
World Health Organization's
assistant director general for
Family and Community Health,
"New HIV Recommendations to
Improve Health, Reduce Infections,
and Save Lives"

HIV/AIDS [human immunodeficiency virus/acquired immune deficiency syndrome] is transmitted by bodily fluids such as blood and semen. It can also be transmitted from mother to child by breast milk. This creates a serious dilemma for mothers who want to raise healthy babies. As the AIDS charity AVERT notes in its article "HIV and Breastfeeding," "For most babies, breastfeeding is without question the best way to be fed, but unfortunately breastfeeding can also transmit HIV. If no antiretroviral drugs are being taken, breastfeeding for two or more years can double the risk of the baby becoming infected to around 40%."

In developed countries, women with HIV are generally advised to avoid feeding their infants breast milk. For example, the US Centers for Disease Control and Prevention (CDC) says on its website, "CDC recommends that infected women in the United States refrain from breastfeeding to avoid postnatal transmission of HIV-1 to their infants through breast milk." The CDC says that even women taking anti-AIDS drugs should not breast-feed their children.

This recommendation makes sense because in the United States, most mothers have access to safe formula and clean water. As a result, feeding children formula instead of breast milk is the safest decision for mothers with HIV.

In developing nations, however, the situation is more complicated. The World Health Organization's (WHO's) report *HIV Transmission Through Breastfeeding: 2007 Update* notes, "Undernutrition is an underlying case of more than half of all deaths in children aged less than five years, and is associated with infectious disease." Breast-feeding helps ensure that children obtain proper nutrition. It also protects children from infected water. Thus, in many situations, it may be safest for HIV-infected women to breast-feed very young infants. WHO therefore stated, "Exclusive breastfeeding is recommended for HIV-infected women for the first six months of life unless replacement feeding [that is, formula or other feeding] meets five criteria—that it is acceptable, feasible, affordable, sustainable, and safe—before that time."

These guidelines were to change, however. Initially, WHO was attempting to discourage mixed feeding, where mothers fed their children breast milk but also supplemented the milk with water or some solid food. Evidence suggested that mixed feeding actually increases the risk of HIV transmission. Therefore, WHO recommended that women feed their children exclusively breast milk for six months, then cease feeding breast milk altogether.

These recommendations, however, proved very difficult to follow. AVERT noted, "In many societies, especially in sub-Saharan Africa, it is normal for a baby to be given water, teas, porridge or other foods as well as breast milk, even during the first few weeks of life." Women who are malnourished are also often concerned that their milk will not be adequate for their children. Thus, in practice, despite WHO recommendations, many women with HIV practiced mixed feeding, giving their infants both breast milk and other food.

Given the prevalence of mixed feeding, WHO altered its recommendations. Now it suggested "for the first time . . . that HIV-positive mothers or their infants take ARVs [antiretroviral drugs, or anti-AIDS drugs] while breastfeeding to prevent HIV transmission," according to a media release on November 30, 2009. WHO encouraged women to continue breast-feeding until the infant was twelve months old as long as the mother or infant was taking antiretroviral drugs.

The switch in WHO policy was enabled in large part by mounting evidence about the relative safety and efficacy of antiretroviral AIDS drugs. For example, a study by Jimmy Volmink et al., published in 2009 by the Cochrane Library, surveyed eighteen trials in sixteen countries with 14,298 participants. "The trials compared the use of antiretrovirals versus placebo, longer regimens versus shorter regimens using the same antiretrovirals, and antiretroviral regimens using different drugs and different durations of treatment. This review of trials found that short courses of certain antiretroviral drugs are effective in reducing mother-to-child transmission of HIV, and are not associated with any safety concerns in the short term." In short, the use of antiretroviral drugs appeared to be effective and safe in preventing the transfer of HIV through breast milk.

Unfortunately, while these drugs work, obtaining access to them can be difficult for many women. For instance, a 2010 study by Putu Duff et al., published in *Journal of the International AIDS Society*, indicated that for women in Uganda, "economic concerns, particularly transport costs from residences to the clinics, represented the greatest barrier to accessing treatment. In addition, HIV-related stigma and non-disclosure of HIV status to clients' sexual partners, long waiting times at the clinic and suboptimal provider-patient interactions at the hospital emerged as significant barriers." The study also found that the women's misconceptions about HIV/AIDS could interfere with treatment. Thus, many women believed that they should not seek treatment until they experienced serious AIDS symptoms. As a result, some did not seek antiretroviral treatment early enough, endangering themselves and their children.

More resources to help women reach and use clinics and more money for education would help to prevent infant infections. Even with these limitations, however, there have been hopeful signs of progress. The *Economist*, in a November 25, 2010, article, noted that the rate of HIV infections worldwide was down from 3.1 million in 2000 to 2.6 million in 2010. The magazine attributed the improvement to changes in behavior such as less promiscuity and more condom use; drug treatments for the infected; and "a big reduction in mother-to-child transmission at birth and during breast-feeding." Preventing the transmission of HIV through breast-feeding, therefore, has been one of the main successes in the fight against AIDS over the last decade.

In *Global Viewpoints: HIV/AIDS*, authors consider other aspects of the worldwide AIDS epidemic in the following chapters: The Spread of the HIV/AIDS Epidemic, Treatment of HIV/AIDS, Moral Issues and HIV/AIDS, and Discrimination and HIV/AIDS. Different viewpoints from around the world express competing perspectives about how to address the issues raised by HIV/AIDS.

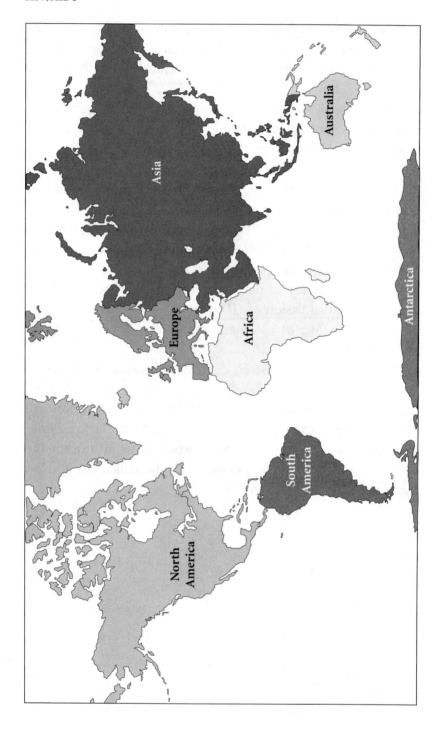

GLOBALVIEWPOINTS

CHAPTER 1

The Spread of the HIV/AIDS Epidemic

The AIDS Plague in the West Is Not Over

Alex Blaze

Alex Blaze, an American living in Paris, is the managing editor of The Bilerico Project, *an LGBTQ (lesbian, gay, bisexual, transgender, and queer) group blog. In the following viewpoint, he argues that the HIV/AIDS epidemic was not ended by the development of anti-AIDS drugs in 1996. Anti-AIDS drugs, he says, are expensive and are not available to many people. He notes that AIDS remains a major threat in the West, especially among gay men. It is also, he notes, an ongoing problem in Africa and other parts of the world. He concludes that it is disingenuous and dangerous to claim that the AIDS crisis is over.*

As you read, consider the following questions:

1. According to Blaze, in 2001 how many twenty-year-old men who had sex with men were affected by HIV?
2. Why does Blaze believe it is puzzling for Sullivan to claim he does not miss AIDS?
3. What did *Romer v. Evans* do, according to Blaze?

Y ou know, I'm falling so far behind in the things that I want to post about that Andrew Sullivan [a writer and blogger] could say that he was right eleven years ago when he said that AIDS is over and I wouldn't even have time to post on it.

Oh wait, that did happen.

AIDS Rates Among Gay Men Remain High

In *The Stranger*'s little parade of mostly white, male queers telling the history of gay rights through the years, Mr. 1996 writes about his infamous article for the *N[ew] Y[ork] Times*, "When Plagues End," where he declared the end of AIDS. He revisits that article by complaining about the "weirdness of the PC [politically correct] mantra" that is responsible for him being "flayed alive."

I suppose that he's now blaming PC for the fact that, in a study last year [2006] by the University of Pittsburgh:

> In 2001, HIV affected about one in twelve 20-year-old MSM [men who have sex with men] in these countries (US, Canada, and Europe). The projected rate of infection could be one in four by the time they are in their thirties, researchers estimated. By age sixty, 58 percent could be infected.

While we don't have to live in absolute fear of the virus... we need to make sure people know why it's important to take basic precautions against it.

Or maybe PC is responsible for the fact that 988,376 Americans were seropositive [that is, tested positive for HIV] in 2005.

Or maybe what really is political correctness's fault is that 29 million people have the virus in sub-Saharan Africa and 40 million do worldwide.

But what's very puzzling is that he says, "I do not miss AIDS." Does it make me a bad person to point out the fact that he is HIV-positive at this point? I'm not stigmatizing people who are seropositive, but it seems rather strange to me that someone would say that they don't miss a disease that they in fact have. Like, of course you don't, it hasn't left.

Sullivan's main point is that since he has the money to afford protease inhibitors developed in 1996 (even though, according to the UN [United Nations], only .0001% of the global population with AIDS has access to antiretroviral drugs) that no one in the world is allowed to try to impress upon people that getting the virus is not something that they want to do. I seriously think it would be great if he flew to Kenya or South Africa to make similar pronouncements about the end of AIDS. While we don't have to live in absolute fear of the virus, and we definitely shouldn't live in fear of the people who have it, if we're going to beat it we have to know where it is and we need to make sure people know why it's important to take basic precautions against it.

It's always a lot easier to ignore a problem than to try and solve it as long as it isn't making your own life inconvenient.

Why Pretend the Epidemic Is Over?

Gabriel Rotello responded to Sullivan's claims over at the *Huffington Post,* and Sullivan responded on his blog. His three basic defenses were that:

a. one can only talk about antiretroviral drugs or prevention, not both;

b. antiretroviral drugs have made the distinction between having HIV and not moot;

c. and telling people about the disease, how to prevent transmission, and the current infection rate will curtail "freedom."

On general principle, I don't respond to blogs, and I think that just pointing out his main points speaks for itself.

So, the real question is, why? Why does he feel the need to say that AIDS is over when it's so clearly not? Well, my theory is that it's always a lot easier to ignore a problem than to try and solve it as long as it isn't making your own life inconvenient. You see that from every corner, whether it be health care (our representatives and senators have great health coverage), racial discrimination (if you're white), or the global warming. In fact, I'd say that's half of what modern conservatism, and 90% of libertarianism/paleo-conservatism, [are] based on, a willful ignorance of all problems affecting anyone else but the person with those political beliefs. So for all the queers who see "liberation" (as Sullivan puts it) in libertarianism, don't be surprised when people of that political stripe ignore any problems that come from queers that might require, you know, money to solve.

But nothing's going to stop him from making erroneous claims. But I do have to wonder why *The Stranger* chose to publish Sullivan's essay instead of one from a more responsible source on the development of antiretroviral drugs. Or maybe they could have published an essay on *Romer v. Evans*, a lawsuit we won that helped prevent many city, county, and municipal anti-discrimination laws from being overturned by state law. Just a thought.

The AIDS Epidemic in Britain Was a Myth

Michael Fitzpatrick

Michael Fitzpatrick is a doctor and the author of The Tyranny of Health: Doctors and the Regulation of Lifestyle. *In the following viewpoint, he argues that warnings of a major HIV/ AIDS epidemic in Britain were seriously and deliberately overstated by AIDS organizations. He says that HIV/AIDS is not sufficiently infectious to have ever presented a real epidemic threat in Britain among mainstream populations. He argues that AIDS organizations chose to try to frighten the entire population to avoid stigmatizing particular groups. He concludes that the result has been a waste of resources.*

As you read, consider the following questions:

1. Who are James Chin and Elizabeth Pisani?
2. According to Fitzpatrick, why has sub-Saharan Africa experienced exceptionally high rates of heterosexually spread HIV infection?
3. What traditional public health methods do Chin and Pisani suggest governments return to?

There is a widely accepted view that Britain was saved from an explosive epidemic of heterosexual AIDS in the late

Michael Fitzpatrick, "The Authorities Have Lied, and I Am Not Glad," *Spiked Review of Books*, August 2008. Copyright © 2008 *Spiked*. Reproduced with permission.

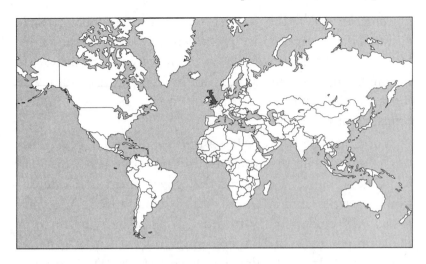

1980s by a bold campaign initiated by gay activists and radical doctors and subsequently endorsed by the government and the mass media.

Doomsday Was Not Imminent

According to advocates of this view, we owe our low rates of HIV infection today largely to the success of initiatives such as the 'Don't Die of Ignorance' leaflet distributed to 23 million households and the scary 'Tombstones and Icebergs' television and cinema adverts (though they are always quick to add that we must maintain vigilance and guard against complacency).

Now former AIDS industry insiders are challenging the imminent heterosexual plague story and many of the other scare stories of the international AIDS panic. James Chin, author of *The AIDS Pandemic: The Collision of Epidemiology with Political Correctness*, is a veteran public health epidemiologist who worked in the World Health Organization's Global Programme on AIDS in the late 1980s and early 1990s. Elizabeth Pisani, a journalist turned epidemiologist and author of *The Wisdom of Whores: Bureaucrats, Brothels and the Business of AIDS*, spent most of the past decade working under the auspices of UNAIDS [the Joint United Nations Programme on HIV/AIDS], which took over the global crusade against HIV in 1996. Once prominent advocates of the familiar doomsday scenarios, both have now turned whistleblowers on their former colleagues in the AIDS bureaucracy, a 'byzantine' world, according to Pisani, in which 'money eclipses truth'.

For Chin, the British AIDS story is an example of a 'glorious myth'—a tale that is 'gloriously or nobly false', but told 'for a good cause'. He claims that government and international agencies, and AIDS advocacy organisations, 'have distorted HIV epidemiology in order to perpetuate the myth of the great potential for HIV epidemics to spread into "general" populations'. In particular, he alleges, HIV/AIDS 'estimates and projections are "cooked" or made up'.

For Chin, the British AIDS story is an example of a 'glorious myth'—a tale that is 'gloriously or nobly false', but told 'for a good cause'.

Manipulating Statistics

While Pisani disputes Chin's claim that UNAIDS epidemiologists deliberately overestimated the epidemic, she admits to what she describes as 'beating up' the figures, insisting—unconvincingly—that there is a 'huge difference' between 'making it up (plain old lying) and beating it up'. Pisani freely acknowledges her role in manipulating statistics to maximise their scare value, and breezily dismisses the 'everyone-is-at-risk nonsense' of the British 'Don't Die of Ignorance' campaign.

Chin's book offers a comprehensive exposure of the hollowness of the claims of the AIDS bureaucracy for the efficacy of their preventive campaigns. He provides numerous examples of how exaggerated claims for the scale of the HIV epidemic (and the risks of wider spread) in different countries and contexts enable authorities to claim the credit for subsequently lower figures, as they 'ride to glory' on curves showing declining incidence. As he argues, 'HIV prevalence is low in most populations throughout the world and can be expected to remain low, not because of effective HIV prevention programmes, but because . . . the vast majority of the world's populations do not have sufficient HIV risk behaviours to sustain epidemic HIV transmission'.

By the late 1980s, it was already clear that, given the very low prevalence of HIV, the difficulty of transmitting HIV through heterosexual sex and the stable character of sexual relationships (even those having multiple partners tend to favour serial monogamy), an explosive HIV epidemic in Britain, of the sort that occurred in relatively small networks of gay men and drug users, was highly improbable, as Don Milligan and I argued in 1987.

Chin's book offers a comprehensive exposure of the hollowness of the claims of the AIDS bureaucracy for the efficacy of their preventive campaigns.

As both Chin and Pisani indicate, high rates of heterosexually spread HIV infection remain the exceptional feature of sub-Saharan Africa (and parts of the Caribbean), where a particular pattern of concurrent networks of sexual partners together with high rates of other sexually transmitted infections facilitated an AIDS epidemic. Though this has had a devastating impact on many communities, Chin suggests that HIV prevalence in sub-Saharan Africa and the Caribbean has been overestimated by about 50 per cent. The good news is that, contrary to the doom-mongering of the AIDS bureaucracy, the rising annual global HIV incidence peaked in the late 1990s and the AIDS pandemic has now passed its peak.

Most significantly, the sub-Saharan pattern has not been replicated in Europe or North America, or even in Asia or

Latin America, though there have been localised epidemics associated with gay men, drug users and prostitution, most recently in South-East Asia and Eastern Europe.

Scaremongering

Many commentators now acknowledge the gross exaggerations and scaremongering of the AIDS bureaucracy. It is clear that HIV has remained largely confined to people following recognised high-risk behaviours, rather than being, in the mantra of the AIDS bureaucracy, a condition of poverty, gender inequality and under-development. Yet they also accept the argument, characterised by Chin as 'political correctness', that it is better to try to terrify the entire population with the spectre of an AIDS epidemic than it is to risk stigmatising the gays and junkies, ladyboys and whores who feature prominently in Pisani's colourful account.

For Chin and Pisani, the main problem of the mendacity of the AIDS bureaucracy is that it leads to misdirected, ineffective and wasteful campaigns to change the sexual behaviour of the entire population, while the real problems of HIV transmission through high-risk networks are neglected. To deal with these problems, both favour a return to traditional public health methods of containing sexually transmitted infections through aggressive testing, contact tracing and treatment of carriers of HIV. Whereas the gay activists who influenced the early approach of the AIDS bureaucracy favoured anonymous and voluntary testing, our whistleblowers now recommend a more coercive approach, in relation to both diagnosis and treatment.

Pisani reminds readers that 'public health is inherently a somewhat fascist discipline' (for example, quarantine restrictions have an inescapably authoritarian character) and enthusiastically endorses the AIDS policies of the Thai military authorities and the Chinese bureaucrats who are not restrained from targeting high-risk groups by democratic niceties. The

AIDS Cannot Reach Epidemic Levels in Most Populations

Since the mid-1990s, I have found myself swimming upstream against mainstream AIDS organizations. I have, during this period, gradually come to the realization that AIDS programs developed by international agencies and faith-based organizations have been and continue to be more socially, politically, and moralistically correct than epidemiologically accurate.

My understanding of how human immunodeficiency virus (HIV) infections are spread (HIV transmission dynamics) and of the very low potential for epidemic transmission in populations with current low HIV prevalence "fits" exactly with what has occurred. However, my conclusions are at marked variance with the beliefs of many AIDS "experts" and with the prevailing Joint United Nations Programme on HIV/AIDS (UNAIDS) paradigm. According to UNAIDS, if effective HIV/AIDS prevention programs are not directed to the general public, especially all youth, epidemic heterosexual HIV transmission will inevitably break out in most populations where HIV epidemics have not yet occurred. My HIV/AIDS paradigm is that *epidemic* HIV transmission requires human behaviors that involve having unprotected sex with *multiple* and *concurrent* sex partners and/or routinely sharing needles and syringes with other injecting drug users (IDU). According to my understanding of HIV transmission dynamics, HIV epidemics cannot occur in populations where high-risk patterns and the highest prevalence of such risk behaviors are not present.

James Chin,
The AIDS Pandemic: The Collision of Epidemiology with Political Correctness. *Oxon, UK: Radcliffe Publishing, 2007.*

problem is that, given the climate of fear generated by two decades of the 'everyone-is-at-risk nonsense', the policy now recommended by Chin and Pisani is likely to lead to more repressive interventions against stigmatised minorities (which will not help to deter the spread of HIV infection).

It is clear that HIV has remained largely confined to people following recognised high-risk behaviours, rather than being, in the mantra of the AIDS bureaucracy, a condition of poverty, gender inequality and underdevelopment.

Chin confesses that he has found it difficult 'to understand how, over the past decade, mainstream AIDS scientists, including most infectious disease epidemiologists, have virtually all uncritically accepted the many "glorious" myths and misconceptions UNAIDS and AIDS activists continue to perpetuate'. An explanation for this shocking betrayal of principle can be found in a 1996 commentary on the British AIDS campaign entitled 'Icebergs and rocks of the "good lie"'. In this article, *Guardian* journalist Mark Lawson accepted that the public had been misled over the threat of AIDS, but argued that the end of promoting sexual restraint (especially among the young) justified the means (exaggerating the risk of HIV infection): as he put it, 'the government has lied and I am glad'.

This sort of opportunism is not confined to AIDS: in other areas where experts are broadly in sympathy with government policy—such as passive smoking, obesity and climate change—they have been similarly complicit in the prostitution of science to propaganda.

It is a pity that Chin and Pisani did not blow their whistles earlier and louder, but better late than never.

Africa's HIV/AIDS Epidemic Is Especially Virulent Because of Poverty

Noel Dzimnenani Mbirimtengerenji

Noel Dzimnenani Mbirimtengerenji is a professor at the College of Public Health at National Taiwan University. In the following viewpoint, he argues that the HIV/AIDS epidemic in sub-Saharan Africa has been so severe in part because of the region's poverty. Women in many parts of Africa, he says, are extremely poor and have little power because of gender discrimination. As a result, they often turn to commercial sex work, resulting in the rapid transmission of HIV/AIDS through the population.

As you read, consider the following questions:

1. According to Mbirimtengerenji, 60 percent of the population of Africa spends less than what per day?

2. In what ways does the author note that poverty-driven sex work carries the risk of unprotected sex?

3. In the author's view, why is becoming an unwilling victim of human trafficking a minor concern for many young women in Africa?

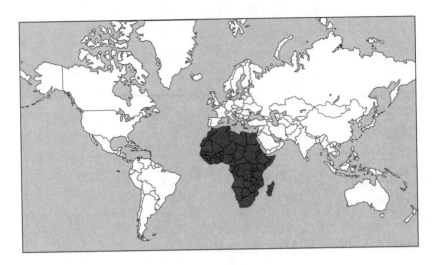

Sub-Saharan Africa is home to 62% of the world's Human Immunodeficiency Virus (HIV) cases, more than 14,000 people are daily infected with the HIV, and 11,000 people are dying daily due to HIV/AIDS-related illnesses. Also, sub-Saharan Africa is home to 70% of the poorest people in the world. This region has the lowest gross domestic product (GDP) in the world, with more than 60% of the population spending less than US $1 a day.

Poverty and AIDS

Poverty includes deprivation, constrained choices, and unfulfilled capabilities, and refers to interrelated features of well-being that impact upon the standard of living and the quality of life. It is not necessarily confined to financial capital, quantified, and minimized in monetary indices [influence]. While financial capital is important, a solely reductionist approach eschews non-monetary resources, the lack of which contributes to and sustains poverty. Many people in sub-Saharan [Africa] are in such poverty. They lack not only money, but assets and skills. Therefore, people strive to get basic needs and mostly [engage in] risky behaviors, such as commercial sex, which can bring basic survival resources.

HIV infection is mostly confined to the poorest, who constitute the most of those infected in Africa. It is not simply that information, education, and counseling activities are unlikely to reach the poor but that such messages are often irrelevant and inoperable given the reality of their lives. Even if the poor understand what they are being urged to do, it is rarely the case that they have either the incentive or the resources to adopt the recommended behaviors.

The capacity of individuals and households to cope with HIV/AIDS depends on their initial endowment of assets—both human and financial. The poorest by definition are least able to cope with the effects of HIV/AIDS, so that immiseration [impoverishment] among the affected populations is increasing. Even the non-poor find their resources diminished by their experience of infection.

It is not simply that information, education, and counseling activities are unlikely to reach the poor but that such messages are often irrelevant and inoperable given the reality of their lives.

Poverty and Sex Work

Many of the poorest are women who often head the poorest households in Africa. Inevitably, such women are often engaged in commercial sexual transactions, sometimes as commercial sexual workers (CSW) but more often, as part of survival strategies for themselves and their dependents. The characteristics of the poor are well known as are some of the causal factors, like early marriage, which contribute to a "culture of poverty,"—the fact that the children of the poor community often become the poor of the succeeding generations. Poverty is also associated with weak endowments of human and financial resources, such as low levels of education with associated low levels of literacy and few marketable skills, generally poor health status and low labor productivity as a result.

However, the consequences of poverty have mostly been associated with migration, sexual trade, polygamy, and teenage marriages. Different research findings have also shown that these variables are directly related to HIV/AIDS. This [viewpoint] illustrates how HIV remains the exact outcome of poverty, with sexual trade, migration, polygamy, and teenage marriages as the predictors in the sub-Saharan region.

Commercial sex workers are perceived to be highly instrumental in the HIV/AIDS pandemic as a high-risk group, reservoir of infection, and bridge into the general population.

The fact that African countries worst affected with HIV/AIDS, such as Botswana and South Africa, are among the most economically developed in the region contradicts the poverty-AIDS argument. However, poverty does seem to be the crucial factor in the spread of HIV/AIDS through sexual trade. The extreme poverty compels most of the young women to [engage in] risky behavior that can easily bring money and resources for survival.

Commercial sex workers are perceived to be highly instrumental in the HIV/AIDS pandemic as a high-risk group, reservoir of infection, and bridge into the general population. Instead of commercial sex work reduction due to HIV/AIDS prevention programs, the trade is gaining ground in Africa.

In sub-Saharan Africa, there is a commercial element in many individual women's sexual relationships, and full-time prostitutes usually operate individually, rather than working as employees. They rent their own room and many women are paid for [sex] on the spot.

Deteriorating economic conditions have caused forced family separation in Zimbabwe. Sexual relationships outside marriage have become the norm for most men in urban areas. Men who work in mines often replace their rural wives with town women, which leads to divorce or reduction in monetary remittances. For women in Zimbabwe, sexual relationships represent the only means of social and economic survival. The traditional subordination of African women places them at disadvantage in terms of their ability to reduce their risk of HIV infection. Separated or divorced women may supplement their low incomes through prostitution.

Commercial sexual exploitation of children is another serious problem, which has the underlying causes in poverty, gender discrimination, war, organized crime, globalization, greed, tradition, and beliefs. Moreover, family dysfunction and the drug trade for women has been an implication of this trade. But among all these factors poverty as a source is featured highly in most African countries. Commercial sexual exploitation of women and trafficking are two elements of the more pervasive problem of sexual abuse that originates from poverty. United Nations Development Programme (UNDP) in their annual report also noted that women victims of poverty are at high risk of unwanted pregnancies and of contracting HIV/AIDS and other sexually transmitted diseases. The minority of children who do manage to escape [the] sex trade face social stigma, family rejection, shame, fear of retribution, and loss of future economic prospects.

In the absence of alternative opportunities to earn a livelihood for themselves and their households, millions of women in Africa indeed sell sex. While millions engage in commercial sex work on a regular basis, even more people not commonly thought of as "commercial sex workers" find themselves needing to exchange sex for money or goods on an occasional basis. Many women have been forced to turn to sexual transactions in order to obtain desperately needed money in com-

HIV/AIDS and Poverty in 20 Sub-Saharan African Countries

Country	% of Population below UN Poverty Line (US $1 a day)	% of People 15–49 with HIV 2005	No of People with HIV (millions)
Swaziland	69	33.4	0.22
Botswana	30	24.1	0.27
Lesotho	49	23.2	0.27
Zimbabwe	80	20.1	1.10
Namibia	56	19.5	0.23
South Africa	50	18.8	5.50
Zambia	86	17.0	1.80
Mozambique	70	16.1	1.80
Malawi	55	14.1	0.94
Central African Republic	57	10.1	0.25
Gabon	NA	7.9	0.06
Cote d'Ivoire	NA	7.1	0.75
Uganda	35	6.7	1.00
Kenya	50	6.1	1.30
Tanzania	51	6.5	1.40
Cameroon	48	5.4	0.51
Congo	NA	5.3	0.21
Nigeria	45	3.9	2.90
Ethiopia	50	3.5	1.30
Guinea Bisau	40	3.5	0.03

TAKEN FROM: Noel Dzimnenani Mbirimtengerenji, "Is HIV/AIDS Epidemic Outcome of Poverty in Sub-Saharan Africa?" *Croation Medical Journal*, 2007.

munities characterized by social inequalities. Some older men with money procure sex from young women in exchange for gifts or money.

Poverty and Condom Use

Moreover, poverty-driven sex work or sexual transactions carry the risk of unprotected sex. People whose livelihood strategies expose them to a high risk of infection are, precisely because they are impoverished, less likely to take seriously the threat of an infection that is fatal in years from the present. They are after all facing the reality of day-to-day survival for themselves and their households. These young girls do not bother to use condoms, as in most cases it is the man who is responsible for that, since he is the one who pays for the sex. Worse still, men are willing to pay exorbitant prices for sex without a condom, which puts women in even greater temptation.

Inequities in gender run parallel to inequities in income and assets. Thus, women are vulnerable not only to HIV/ AIDS infection but also to the economic impact of HIV/ AIDS.

In addition to these findings, it was also reported that poverty was a key cause to commercial sex work in Swaziland. Almost a third of commercial sex workers in this country were employed and undertook commercial sex work to supplement their income.

Sechaba Consultants in South Africa also identified poverty as a significant factor in commercial sex work. The prevalence rate in this country was 33.4% by the end of 2005. However, the transition from employment in garment factories to commercial sex work, in order to increase the income, was a form of upward mobility for some commercial sex workers who primarily tended to provide sexual services to foreigners.

There are two groups of commercial sex workers in Swaziland—those mainly providing sexual services for the local Basotho and those providing sexual services mainly to foreigners. The latter included schoolgirls and school dropouts who became involved in commercial sex work to support their families. It was claimed that foreigners were always ready to pay more than local customers, particularly when they did not use condoms.

Malawi is losing a lot of highly trained and experienced professionals to HIV/AIDS. In this country, where the adult HIV/AIDS prevalence is 12.2%, government has been advised to take pro-active steps to institute appropriate policies to control the impact of the deadly pandemic by prohibiting women's commercial sex work. Kumbanyiwa added that despite the law that prohibits commercial sex work in the country, there are many prostitutes who are exacerbating the HIV/AIDS problem. If sex workers did not have lucrative clientele who sometimes pay in US dollars, they could not have been lining up along the cities' streets every night. Indeed most of the people in Malawi who are dying from the scourge are young energetic women and men who could assist in the development.

In fact, there are a number of interlocking reasons why most women are more exposed to commercial sex and vulnerable to HIV/AIDS than men. The major reasons for commercial sex include female physiology, women's lack of power to negotiate sexual relationships with male partners, especially in marriage, and the gendered nature of poverty, with poor women being particularly vulnerable. Inequities in gender run parallel to inequities in income and assets. Thus, women are vulnerable not only to HIV/AIDS infection but also to the economic impact of HIV/AIDS. This is often a result of gendered power relations evident in rural households, which can leave women prone to the infection of HIV. With increasing economic insecurity, women become vulnerable to sexual harassment and exploitation at and beyond the workplace, and to trading in sexual activities to secure income for household needs.

Food Shortages and Teenage Prostitution

According to IRIN News, the ongoing drought has left hundreds of thousands in eastern Kenya facing severe food shortages and has driven many rural people into towns in search of work and food. Young women are sent from deep within the interior to the roadside to sell honey and homemade crafts. IRIN News added that parents have resorted to sending their young daughters into the towns to trade their bodies for money to feed their families. It has been noted that women find a ready market in towns like Makindu, where truck drivers welcome their company in the bars and in their beds. The result of this potent mix of sex with multiple partners and excessive alcohol consumption is that Makindu in Kenya has an HIV prevalence rate almost double that of the general population. In this country, where the HIV/AIDS prevalence is now 6.1%, women are well organized for commercial sex as there is flourishing tourism.

Many girls in Malindi, Kenya, as soon as they have breasts, find European boyfriends. It was added that, because of poverty, the community has embraced commercial sex as a way of improving their living standards.

The tradition of early marriage among Mijikenda, the nine linguistically related ethnic groups who inhabit the Kenyan coastal districts of Kilifi, Kwale, Malindi, and Mombasa, could be contributing to the problem of teenage prostitution.

It has been documented that poverty causes sex trafficking as well, because women have no other choice but to accept to be exported to another land where basic resources are easily found. [A way to put] an end to this exploitative practice is to offer viable economic options for poverty-stricken women and girls.

The fact that sex trafficking is a direct product of poverty is widely recognized by humanitarian organizations, governments, and academic researchers. The United States Agency for International Development pointed [out] in their 2005 annual report that trafficking is inextricably linked to poverty. Wherever deprivation and economic hardship prevail, there will be those destitute and desperate enough to enter into the fraudulent employment schemes that are the most common intake systems in the world of trafficking, let alone spreading the HIV/AIDS epidemic.

Because of poverty, the community has embraced commercial sex as a way of improving their living standards.

It has to be further made clear that the real danger of becoming an unwilling victim of human trafficking syndicates and commercial sex turns into a minor concern of a young woman who is desperate enough to hoist and relieve her family from the vicious cycle of poverty. These young women have illusions and dreams that frequently prevail over life's sad realities, especially in the youthful mind of someone very eager to escape from material deprivation. Many are prepared to face any form of consequences if only to free their families from the clutches and bondage of poverty.

Therefore, it is a natural fact that commercial sex is an indisputable indicator of poverty and the fatal predictor of deadly HIV/AIDS.

Africa's HIV/AIDS Epidemic Is Especially Virulent Because It Was First

John Iliffe

John Iliffe is professor of African history at the University of Cambridge. In the following viewpoint, he argues that the HIV/AIDS epidemic in Africa has been especially virulent because the disease came to Africa first and became established in the general population before it was discovered. He suggests that Africa's massive population growth probably also helped to exacerbate the disease. Factors like poverty and sexual traditions, which are often blamed for Africa's epidemic, were contributing factors, he says, but they were of secondary importance overall.

As you read, consider the following questions:

1. What were the most common types of earlier epidemics in Africa's history, according to Iliffe?

2. According to the author, when did population growth peak in sub-Saharan Africa, and what was the growth rate at that time?

3. How does Iliffe say the global depression of the 1970s exacerbated the AIDS epidemic in Africa?

John Iliffe, "Causation: A Synthesis," *The African AIDS Epidemic: A History*, Athens, OH: Ohio University Press, 2006, pp. 58–64. Copyright © 2006 Ohio University Press.

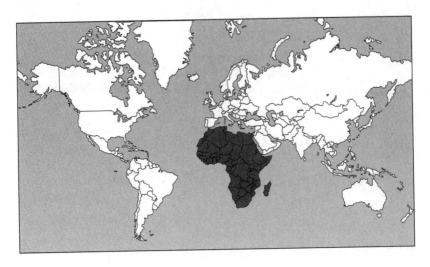

It is time to return to [South African] President [Thabo] Mbeki's question: Why has Africa had the world's most terrible HIV/AIDS epidemic? An answer must bring together the nature of the virus, the historical sequence of its global expansion, and the circumstances into which it spread, giving particular weight among those circumstances to gender inequalities, sexual behaviour, and impoverishment. Many existing answers perhaps concentrate too exclusively on the circumstances, arguing for the primary importance of either sexual behaviour or poverty.

A Catastrophe in Slow Motion

The distinctive features of HIV as a virus were that it was relatively difficult to transmit, it killed almost all those it infected (unless [persons were] kept alive by antiretroviral drugs), it killed them slowly after a long incubation period, it remained infectious throughout its course, it showed few symptoms until its later stages, and when symptoms appeared they were often those common to the local disease environment. This unique combination of features gave a unique character to the epidemic, 'a catastrophe in slow motion' spreading silently for many years before anyone recognised its existence. One consequence was that whatever part of the world had the first such epidemic would suffer especially severely, for the epidemic would have time to establish itself, unseen, not only in many people over a large area but in the general heterosexual population, where it would be vastly more difficult to contain than in some limited high-risk group contracting the disease through the initial infection of individuals whose distinctive behaviour patterns had brought them into contact with it.

Thus the fundamental reason why Africa had the worst AIDS epidemic was because it had the first AIDS epidemic. Understandably, many Africans were initially unwilling to accept this, rejecting the notion that HIV evolved from SIV [simian immunodeficiency virus, a disease of monkeys and apes] within Africa, despite the powerful evidence for it, because they felt that it was a racial slur—as indeed some commentators intended it to be. To deny the origin of the disease, however, was to deny oneself an understanding of the particular tragedy that had struck the continent.

One way of grasping the uniqueness of HIV/AIDS is to contrast it with earlier epidemics in African history. These were of three types. The most common were highly infectious diseases that swept briefly through large populations, swiftly killing susceptible people before burning out and becoming quiescent until the next epidemic. Smallpox, an ancient African disease, was of this type, as were cholera, an Asian disease that spread to Africa in several nineteenth-century epidemics, and the great influenza pandemic of 1918—'three-day flu', as it was known in South Africa—that killed between two and five per cent of the population in most parts of Africa. All these epidemics clearly differed from HIV/AIDS in their greater infectiousness, their short incubation period, the speed with which they killed, and their brief but dramatic impact, which provoked equally dramatic human responses. Somewhat different were diseases with endemic reservoirs in African animals, from which they were transmitted to human beings by insect vectors, sometimes in epidemic proportions. This was true of plague [transmitted through flea bites], which especially infected North Africa from the fourteenth-century Black Death to the nineteenth century; malaria and yellow fever, both mosquito-borne diseases that became epidemic in specific natural conditions; and sleeping sickness, an endemic disease of wild game transmitted to human beings in epidemic form by tsetse flies as a result of disturbance of the natural environment during the early colonial period. HIV, too, had its natural reservoir, but was far more difficult to transmit as a human disease, was not carried by an insect vector, and consequently, once established in humans, was independent of the natural environment and free to spread throughout the continent. In that respect, HIV/AIDS was more like two other diseases that also began as epidemics but became endemic, venereal syphilis and tuberculosis, both diseases of uncertain history that probably became widespread in inland regions of Africa only during the late nineteenth and twentieth centuries. They differed from HIV, however, in that they were easier to transmit, had more visible symptoms once established, but were less often fatal.

The fundamental reason why Africa had the worst AIDS epidemic was because it had the first AIDS epidemic.

Timing and Mobility

These contrasts demonstrate the distinctiveness of HIV/AIDS as a disease, which shaped not only the progress of the epidemic but also, as will be seen, the ways in which Africans understood and reacted to it. Yet the comparison also reveals one common factor of all these epidemics (except perhaps plague once it was established in North Africa): that epidemics are intimately related to mobility, whether the clustering together of people in drought or famine that so often caused smallpox outbreaks, the human disturbance of the natural environment that precipitated epidemic sleeping sickness, the movement of returning soldiers along shipping lanes and railway lines that spread the great influenza, or the migration routes along which southern African mineworkers carried tuberculosis to their rural homes. In this respect the HIV epidemic was fully in the pattern of past epidemics.

A contrast with earlier African epidemics demonstrates the importance of HIV's distinctiveness as a virus. A contrast with other HIV epidemics demonstrates why it was so important for Africa that it had the first. During the 1990s it became clear that the epidemics that had begun in the United States and Europe during the late 1970s were unlikely to reach African dimensions. Once imported, both had taken root first among homosexuals and injecting drug users (IDUs), partly self-segregated groups quickly targeted by health services and bearing a stigma that helped to sensitise the general population to the danger of contracting HIV. The North American epidemic did spread among heterosexuals from poor urban minority groups, but they too were significantly differentiated from the bulk of the population, and in the meantime antiretroviral drugs had become available. Latin American epidemics generally fell into the same pattern. Greater international concern centred on the possibility that infections in Asia or Eastern Europe might expand into generalised heterosexual epidemics of the African type. All these, however, had begun among restricted groups of IDUs, homosexuals, commercial sex workers, or their clients. In Thailand and Kampuchea, early areas of concern, it proved possible to contain epidemics by targeting these groups, much as South Africa largely contained its initial epidemic among white homosexuals. India, China, and Russia were seen as the danger points for a 'second wave' of HIV, but sceptics pointed out that few antenatal [prenatal] clinics outside Africa (and Haiti) showed HIV prevalence of more than 1 per cent and that in Asia, at least, casual and intergenerational sex concentrated almost entirely on institutionalised commercial sex workers who could be targeted. The important point, it was agreed, was for governments to intervene at the earliest stage of an epidemic. This was the opportunity that Africa had not enjoyed.

Demographic Factors

Thus the origin and nature of the virus primarily determined the character of the African epidemic. But it was shaped also by the multitude of circumstances in which it took place, many of them with roots far back in the past. No one of these was decisive; all must be incorporated into an explanation. The most fundamental was the demographic context. Before the twentieth century, Africa's hostile disease environment, harsh physical and climatic conditions, and history of exploitation had made it an underpopulated continent. During the twentieth century medical and other innovations had removed many of these constraints and population had grown at increasing pace, perhaps multiplying six or seven times in the course of the century. Growth peaked in the 1980s, when the population of sub-Saharan Africa grew at about 3.1 per cent per year, almost certainly the fastest natural increase over a long period for any large population in human history. It cannot have been entirely coincidental that HIV became epidemic at exactly the moment when demographic growth reached its peak. One long-term connection was the pressure that lay behind the penetration of the forest, exposing human beings to animal diseases of which SIV was only one. More immediately, population growth drove Africa's massive late-twentieth century urbanisation—at about 5 per cent per year during the 1980s—which created cities like Kinshasa and Abidjan, where networks of partner exchange were wide enough to raise HIV to epidemic levels. Later, in the 1990s, emerging areas of rural overpopulation and poverty, such as Malawi, would provide conditions for especially devastating epidemic impact. In both town and country, rapid demographic growth swelled in particular the numbers of young people who were especially vulnerable to HIV. In the mid 1990s, for example, one-third of all Tanzanians were aged between 10 and 24. One reason why HIV spread more widely in Africa than elsewhere was this preponderance of young people.

The epidemic also came at a particular moment in Africa's medical history. The leading historian of HIV/AIDS, Mirko Grmek, suggested that the epidemic was, paradoxically, in part a consequence of medical advance: that until medicine had reduced the prevalence of other infectious diseases such as tuberculosis and smallpox, death rates were too high to allow HIV to establish itself in sufficient numbers of people to reach epidemic proportions. There is no obvious way to test this intriguing suggestion, which perhaps exaggerates the extent of medical advance in sub-Saharan Africa, where in the early 1990s communicable diseases still caused 71 per cent of morbidity. Nevertheless, it is both true and disturbing that the epidemic followed immediately on the period of greatest medical improvement in the continent's history. Between 1965 and 1988, life expectancy at birth in sub-Saharan Africa rose from 45 to 51 years. Over the same period the ratio of doctors to population increased by about 50 per cent and the ratio of nurses to population more than doubled. In 1974 the World Health Organization launched its Expanded Programme on Immunisation, in 1977 it completed the eradication of smallpox, and in 1978 it adopted a global strategy of primary health care. Some have suggested that smallpox vaccination or polio immunisation may have spread HIV. Neither is likely, but it is possible that massive use of injections may have contributed to the HIV-2 epidemic in Guinea-Bissau and helped to adapt HIV-1 to human hosts, while blood transfusion was a significant factor in transmitting the virus early in the epidemic. On the other hand, medical advance—especially prior research into viral cancer—enabled scientists to identify HIV and its natural history with extraordinary speed and precision once the epidemic attracted attention. Had it occurred twenty years earlier, the response, as one specialist put it, might have been mere 'thrashing about'.

In both town and country, rapid demographic growth swelled in particular the numbers of young people who were especially vulnerable to HIV.

Migration and Sexual Behavior

In Grmek's analysis, the technology that identified HIV was, ironically, part of the same technology that enabled it to flourish. He had in mind especially the advances in transport and human mobility that carried HIV to all parts of the African continent and the world. As with influenza and tuberculosis, mobile people spread HIV along their networks of communication and gave the epidemic the shape of the commercial economy, whether they were migrants taking the disease to rural Karonga, fishermen spreading it around the shores of Lake Victoria, long-distance drivers infecting Beitbridge and Berberati, or sex workers and labourers carrying the virus from Abidjan to savanna towns and villages. Everywhere infection concentrated along motor roads, which were especially central in Africa because its transport system largely postdated the age of railway building. Some have argued that HIV/AIDS could not have become an epidemic disease before the existence of widespread motor transport, but that seems doubtful, for many diseases with shorter incubation periods spread their infection across continents in pre-modern times. Yet the high infection levels in Côte d'Ivoire and the association between oscillating migration and rural prevalence in Central Africa can leave no doubt of the importance of migrant labour and the regional inequalities underlying it in fuelling the epidemic.

Gender inequalities and sexual behaviour are among the most important and controversial of the circumstances shap-

AIDS in Sub-Saharan Africa

AIDS was first reported in human populations over 20 years ago [around 1988]. The human immunodeficiency virus was isolated within a few years of the first human case report, and drugs that can prolong the lives of people infected with HIV have been available for over ten years. Despite this rapid progress, a vaccine remains elusive and most of the people in the world who are infected with HIV face significant hurdles to obtain effective treatment. In North America and Western Europe, HIV infection rates were highest among men having sex with men and injection drug users. By contrast, HIV transmission in Africa and Asia is primarily via heterosexual intercourse. The highest prevalence countries are among the world's poorest and most are located in sub-Saharan Africa.

The 2006 Report on the global AIDS epidemic from UNAIDS (May 2006) reported that 23.6 million of the 36.3 million people globally living with HIV/AIDS are living in sub-Saharan Africa and that almost 70% of the 2.8 million deaths due to HIV/AIDS in 2005 occurred in sub-Saharan Africa. While the epidemic's dynamics are changing and incidence (new infection rates) rising in Asia and Eastern Europe, the sheer numbers of affected people in sub-Saharan Africa mean that HIV/AIDS will remain a powerful determinant of health and development in this region for the foreseeable future.

Matthew Hodge,
"HIV/AIDS, Demographics, and Economic Development,"
in HIV/AIDS in Africa: Challenges & Impact,
eds. Edith Mukudi Omwami, Stephen Commins,
and Edmond J. Keller. Trenton, NJ:
Africa World Press, 2008, pp. 8–9.

ing the epidemic. Early observers often attributed the scale of infection in Africa to high levels of sexual promiscuity. A survey in 1989–90 in eight mainland African states and three Asian countries (including Sri Lanka and Thailand) questioned this and suggested a more complicated situation. It found that most African men had had sex during the previous year only with their regular partner and that only small percentages had had five or more casual partners. 'Non-marital sex,' the enquiry concluded, 'is a relatively rare event for a majority of men and women'. The survey also showed that the difference in each country between rural and urban sexual behaviour was relatively small: A more important distinction may have been that urban sexual networks were wider. On the other hand, when compared with Sri Lanka, a country of severe restraint, African sexual behaviour was less inhibited: men and women began sex earlier, married earlier, had wider age differentials between husband and wife, and more often had pre-marital, casual, and commercial sex, a pattern that anthropologists attributed to the absence in Africa of the land scarcity that led Asian families to guard their women jealously, to Africa's polygynous traditions that encouraged men to seek multiple partners without linking sexual partnership to age, and to the twentieth century social changes—especially longer intervals between sexual debut and marriage—that encouraged pre-marital sex in areas as diverse as Kinshasa, Bangui, Kampala, Botswana, Soweto, Yorubaland, and southern Senegal.

When the survey compared African sexual behaviour with that in Thailand, however, a more complex picture emerged. Thailand shared Sri Lanka's restrictive sexual attitude towards most women but not towards men, so that Thai men were as sexually active as African men but concentrated their non-marital sex almost entirely on commercial sex workers. As has been seen, this was true in only a minority of African areas: in Rwanda, Burundi, urban Ethiopia and Senegal, and to some degree in cities with large male majorities like Nairobi. Moreover, Africa's entrepreneurial sex workers seldom worked in brothels, which made them more difficult to target with preventive measures than their counterparts in Thailand and elsewhere in Asia.

Gender inequalities and sexual behaviour are among the most important and controversial of the circumstances shaping the epidemic.

Four additional circumstances created opportunities for HIV infection in Africa. One was the widespread prevalence of sexually transmitted diseases, especially the global epidemic of HSV-2 [a herpes virus] that by the early 2000s doubled the risk of HIV infection for 70 per cent or more of the population in many regions. Another—still unproven but strongly suspected—was the lack of male circumcision in large parts of eastern and southern Africa that helped to explain especially high HIV prevalence there. The third, with a similar regional impact, was the lack of economic opportunities for women, especially in eastern and southern cities, which weakened their ability to protect themselves against infection. Added to that, a fourth circumstance was the frequent disparity of age between partners resulting both from female poverty and polygynous traditions, which was of central importance in transmitting disease between age groups. Ironically, a major feature of precolonial African societies, the rarity of endogenous social strata [that is, the fact that there is sexual contact across different social classes], made them especially vulnerable to HIV. Thus although African sexual behaviour was far from the generalised promiscuity of Western myth, it contributed in important ways to the scale of the epidemic. The best proof of this would be the role that behavioural change would later play in reducing infection.

Poverty's Role

Poverty was the other major circumstance shaping the epidemic, but again its impact was far from simple. HIV/AIDS was not in any sense a 'quintessential disease of poverty'. Africa did not have a more terrible epidemic than India because it was poorer but because it was infected first. At the national level, HIV did not target the poorest countries, as high prevalence in Botswana and other parts of southern Africa demonstrated. At the social level, the most striking point was the wide range of people infected. 'HIV affects ordinary people,' wrote Noerine Kaleeba, founder of The AIDS Support Organisation in Uganda. 'It does not only affect "the poor". It does not only affect "the affluent". It affects a cross-section of people.' One indication of this was that blame for the epidemic was seldom allocated on grounds of economic class. The pattern seen in Karonga, where infection was associated with mobility, education, and off-farm employment, was common early in the epidemic, but not universal. At Kabarole in western Uganda in 1991–3, for example, people aged 15–24 with secondary schooling were more than twice as likely to be infected than the uneducated, but the first attempt in Masaka to relate infection to categories of wealth, measured by household property ownership, found that 'both male and female heads of the poorest households were most likely to be HIV positive'.

A nuanced picture emerged from the most careful study, in Kisumu in western Kenya in 1996, using a composite index of education, occupation, and household possessions to define socio-economic status. It found that among men over 25 there was no association between this status and HIV prevalence, among men aged 15–24 and women over 25 higher socio-economic status was associated with somewhat higher HIV prevalence, but among women aged 15–24 prevalence was highest among those with low socio-economic status. The poorer women had wider age differentials from their husbands, were less likely to use condoms, and had higher rates of HSV-2. Poverty, it appeared, did not give birth to HIV, but it was an effective incubator.

Africa did not have a more terrible epidemic than India because it was poorer but because it was infected first.

South Africa's population survey of 2002 found a strong concentration of the disease in informal urban locations but no statistically significant association between infection and household poverty, suggesting that social environment was more important than mere income. One connection was probably the prevalence of other sexually transmitted diseases, as in Kisumu. A second was the greater poverty of women. Others may have been malnutrition and parasite infestation that increased susceptibility to disease and the likelihood of perinatal transmission, although research in this field was still at an early stage. More visible were the effects of poverty in making progress from AIDS to death so much faster in Africa than in developed countries, owing to greater exposure to opportunistic infections and less access to medical remedies—especially, after 1996, to antiretroviral drugs. Most visible and distressing of all was that poverty accentuated the suffering of AIDS patients bereft of the most elementary palliative care.

This was the point where Africa's poverty added so greatly to the scale of the epidemic. After significant economic growth and medical advance in most regions for thirty years after the Second World War, the global depression of the late 1970s that reversed Africa's fortunes coincided exactly with the transformation of HIV into an epidemic disease. The depression exposed African regimes that were over-extended, over-staffed, and over-borrowed. Between 1965 and 1980 sub-Saharan Africa's real Gross Domestic Product had grown at 4.2 per cent a year; between 1980 and 1990 it grew at only 2.1 per cent a year, or only two-thirds of the rate of population growth. During the 1980s per capita health spending more than halved in the poorest countries. Heavily indebted regimes seeking international support had to accept structural adjustment programmes demanding still further economy on services, including user fees at medical institutions that did less to raise money than to deter the poor from using them. In Zambia utilisation of urban health centres fell by 80 per cent. Instead patients turned to indigenous healers, while biomedical doctors and their wealthier patients retreated to private practice. This was the context within which Africans and their governments faced the first and worst of HIV epidemics.

Senegal Controlled Its AIDS Epidemic

United States Agency for International Development

The United States Agency for International Development (USAID) is the US federal agency primarily responsible for administering civilian foreign aid. In the following viewpoint, the organization reports on Senegal's battle against the AIDS epidemic. USAID notes that Senegal has had substantial success in fighting HIV/AIDS. Its aggressive government response to the epidemic included promotion of condom use, educational efforts, and the involvement of religious and community leaders. While HIV/AIDS remains a serious problem in Senegal, USAID concludes, the government's quick and vigorous response has helped increase awareness and condom use and has significantly lowered the rate of infection and death.

As you read, consider the following questions:

1. In 2007, what percentage of the adult population in Senegal had HIV, and how many cases of HIV were there in Senegal, according to the report?

2. What reason does USAID give for the high condom use among sex workers and the general population in Senegal?

3. How have Muslim religious leaders in Senegal contributed to AIDS prevention, according to USAID?

United States Agency for International Development, "Senegal: HIV/AIDS Health Profile," September 2010.

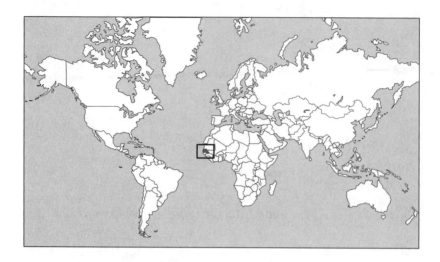

Senegal is considered to be one of the world's success stories in HIV prevention. While other sub-Saharan African countries are experiencing the worst generalized epidemics in the world, Senegal maintains one of the lowest HIV prevalence levels on the continent and has a concentrated epidemic. The primary reasons for Senegal's success at minimizing the spread of the disease are the country's conservative sexual norms and active engagement by the public and private sectors ever since the first emergence of HIV/AIDS in the mid-1980s. In 2007, 1 percent of the adult population was HIV positive, and the Joint United Nations Programme on HIV/AIDS (UNAIDS) estimates that Senegal had 67,000 cases of HIV.

Concentration of the Epidemic

HIV/AIDS in Senegal is concentrated in most-at-risk populations (MARPs). Infection rates are highest among female commercial sex workers (CSWs), with rates as high as 19.8 and 29 percent recorded in 2006 in Dakar and Ziguinchor, respectively. Rates are also high among men who have sex with men (MSM); in 2004, 21.5 percent were HIV positive in Dakar according to UNAIDS. In the general population, prevalence rates vary on a regional basis, according to the International

HIV and AIDS in Senegal

Population Characteristic	Figures for Senegal
Total population	14.1 million (mid-2010)
Estimated population living with HIV/AIDS	67,000 [47,000–96,000] (end 2007)
Adult HIV prevalence	1.0% [0.7–1.4%] (end 2007)
HIV prevalence in most-at-risk populations	Female sex workers: 19.8% (Dakar) (2006) 29.0% (Ziguinchor) (2006) MSM: [Men who have sex with men] 21.5% (Dakar) (2004)
Percentage of HIV-infected people receiving antiretroviral therapy	56% (end 2007)

TAKEN FROM: "Senegal: HIV/AIDS Health Profile," United States Agency for International Development, September 2010. http://www.usaid.gov.

HIV/AIDS Alliance, and reach as high as 2.8 percent and 2.35 percent, in Kolda and Ziguinchor, respectively, the regions that border Guinea-Bissau to the south.

According to the 2008 United Nations General Assembly Special Session (UNGASS) report, approximately two women are HIV positive for every HIV-positive man. This feminization of the epidemic is a sharp shift from the beginning of the epidemic, when the numbers of HIV-positive men were higher. Women 25 to 29 years of age now have the highest prevalence of any age group at 1.5 percent, according to the 2005 Senegal Demographic and Health Survey (SDHS), with the next highest group, men 35 to 39 years of age, at 0.7 percent.

Children in Senegal are affected by the epidemic by contracting HIV from their mothers and by losing a parent to AIDS. In 2007, there were 8,400 children under age 18 who had been orphaned by AIDS and 3,100 children under the age of 15 living with HIV according to UNAIDS. The majority of these children have no extended family networks to rely on following the death of their parents. The elderly have also been affected by the AIDS-related deaths of adult children who had previously supported them.

Because of public-private prevention efforts, condom use among sex workers and the general population is high—three times greater than it was a decade ago, according to UNAIDS. Still, challenges to continued success in containing the epidemic remain, including population movement across borders, early sexual debut, and high HIV prevalence among sex workers and MSM. Moreover, a large proportion of MSM also have sex with women, thus providing a bridge of transmission to the general population. In 2002, 88 percent of MSM in Dakar reported having had vaginal sex, according to UNAIDS. Lack of knowledge about HIV status is another concern; less than 2 percent of individuals know their serological status [that is, whether they have HIV], according to Senegal's 2008 UNGASS report.

The national program undertook significant measures . . . including condom promotion, sentinel surveillance, confidential counseling and testing, education of sex workers, and integration of HIV into sex education.

People living with HIV are particularly vulnerable to developing drug-resistant tuberculosis (TB) because of their increased susceptibility to infection and progression to active TB. Furthermore, TB is one of the main causes of death for people living with HIV. Senegal has a high TB burden, with an incidence of 280 per 100,000 population in 2008, according to the World Health Organization (WHO). In 2008, the percentage of new adult TB patients who were HIV positive was 6.9 percent; co-infection with HIV and TB complicates the care and treatment of both diseases.

National Response

The Government of Senegal responded rapidly to HIV/AIDS, establishing in 1986 the *Programme National de Lutte Contre le SIDA* (National Program for the Fight against AIDS), which in 2002 was renamed the *Conseil National de Lutte Contre le SIDA* (National Council for the Fight against AIDS). The national program undertook significant measures to prevent HIV/AIDS transmission, including condom promotion, sentinel surveillance, confidential counseling and testing, education of sex workers, and integration of HIV into sex education. The current national strategic plan, *Le Plan Stratégigue de Lutte contre le SIDA (PSLS) 2007–2011*, was built on the 2002–2006 PSLS and continues successful HIV prevention programs.

Senegal's 2002–2006 strategy emphasized a multisectoral approach that included the participation of government ministries, the private sector, and religious and other civil society organizations, as well as PLWHA [people living with HIV/AIDS]. Priority action areas included prevention, blood safety, sexually transmitted infections, mother-to-child transmission, and social mobilization. The 2007–2011 strategic plan continues to prioritize these action areas to maintain Senegal's low HIV prevalence. HIV/AIDS prevention is part of the strategic aims of all of Senegal's various development planning programs, including the Poverty Reduction Strategic Papers for 2002–2015 and the Education and Training Development Program for 2000–2010. The government provides free antiretroviral therapy (ART) to those in need. As of 2007, 56 percent of PLWHA were receiving ART according to WHO/UNAIDS/UNICEF [United Nations Children's Fund].

Involving Leaders and Institutions

From the start of the epidemic, the government involved religious and community leaders in HIV prevention. In 1992, the Catholic Church formed *SIDA Service*, an organization to support and care for people living with HIV/AIDS (PLWHA).

The organization remains active to this day, working to combat stigma and discrimination against PLWHA; *SIDA Service* has grown to 500 volunteers and employees across 23 branches throughout Senegal. At a 1995 national conference, Muslim and Christian religious leaders proclaimed support for HIV prevention activities and committed to working with health care providers responding to the disease. This led to the development of a national prevention strategy that combines outreach programs targeting MARPs with efforts by religious leaders and faith-based organizations to reinforce traditional sexual norms, including monogamy. Muslim religious leaders, in particular, have been at the forefront of the national response, delivering sermons about HIV/AIDS in mosques and incorporating AIDS education into religious teaching programs. Both Muslim and Christian organizations provide care and psychosocial services to promote tolerance.

From the start of the epidemic, the government involved religious and community leaders in HIV prevention.

The role of public-private partnerships (PPPs) in combating HIV/AIDS has become increasingly important; using business expertise and resources was identified as one of the major steps in reducing the number of new infections throughout Africa. In Senegal, there has been increased private sector involvement in HIV/AIDS prevention and treatment in recent years. The number of private companies signed onto the ILO [International Labour Organization] Charter on HIV within the workplace increased from 65 companies in 2006 to 445 in 2009. An additional 99 private sector companies are implementing HIV interventions through joint agreements with coalitions of private companies and artisan trade unions.

The Global Fund to Fight AIDS, Tuberculosis and Malaria has disbursed $28 million in Senegal since 2003 to support HIV prevention and treatment programs, primarily through the National AIDS Council. Recently, Senegal was approved for a $39.7 million, ninth-round grant for HIV/AIDS programs. The U.S. Government (USG) provides nearly 30 percent of the Global Fund's total contributions.

The Epidemic in the Philippines Has Been Less Virulent than Expected

Eugenio M. Caccam Jr.

Eugenio M. Caccam Jr. is associate director of Philippine Business for Social Progress. In the following viewpoint, he argues that the Philippines has been spared the worst of the AIDS epidemic, perhaps because of its culture and geography. He notes, however, that the crisis may be worse than thought because of underreporting. Also, he argues that there are dangerous signs of HIV spread among at-risk groups such as gay men, intravenous drug users, sex workers, and overseas Filipino workers. Caccam concludes that if preventive steps are not taken, AIDS rates in the Philippines could increase rapidly, resulting in a full-blown epidemic.

As you read, consider the following questions:

1. What geographical factors does Caccam suggest may have kept HIV/AIDS rates low in the Philippines?

2. The vulnerability of migrant workers to HIV/AIDS is determined and influenced by what factors, according to the author?

Eugenio M. Caccam Jr., "The Philippines: Current State and Future Projections of the Spread of HIV/AIDS," *Fighting a Rising Tide: The Response to AIDS in East Asia*, edited by Tadashi Yamamoto and Satoko Itoh, Tokyo: Japan Center for International Exchange, 2006, pp. 207–209, 212–218, 223. Copyright © Japan Center for International Exchange, 2006. All rights reserved. Reproduced by permission.

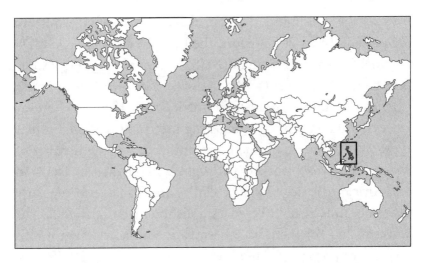

3. What does the Fourth AIDS Medium Term Plan seek to do to maintain the low incidence of AIDS in the Philippines?

Health experts have described the prevalence and growth of HIV/AIDS in the Philippines as low and slow. Since 1984, when the first case of HIV/AIDS was documented with the death of a foreign national, there has been, as of March 2005, an incidence of only 0.01%, or 2,250 cases in a population of nearly 85 million. To the average layperson, the figure is not a source of concern, especially when compared with the figures of some neighboring Asian countries or when set side by side with the more daunting figures of two other communicable diseases, tuberculosis (TB) and malaria. According to the Department of Health (DOH), TB kills 75 Filipinos every day; while figures from the World Health Organization (WHO) showed that there were 43,644 malaria cases registered in the Philippines in 2003 alone.

Dangerous Conditions Are Present

Local and international experts have been baffled by the low prevalence and slow growth of HIV/AIDS in the Philippines because the conditions that can make the situation explosive are present. In its 2002 report, the DOH's National HIV/AIDS Sentinel Surveillance System (NHSSS) attempted to offer some possible explanations: (a) the network of sex workers is not as extensive as those found in countries with high HIV prevalence; (b) the rate of injecting drug use is low, although other types of drug use might be more prevalent; (c) the number of clients seen by sex workers per night is lower than in Thailand and Africa; (d) social hygiene clinics are available to regularly examine and treat infected establishment-based female sex workers; and (e) there have been early and accelerated multi-sectoral responses mounted against the threat of HIV/AIDS. The report says that the low rate of prevalence may also mean that the virus has not yet reached the critical level in the population to promote a rapid spread, and it is believed that the disease is concentrated in vulnerable groups.

The low figures might also be the result of inadequate data capture, as reporting is done primarily through a passive surveillance system, the HIV/AIDS Registry, which logs chiefly Western blot-confirmed HIV cases reported by hospitals, blood banks, laboratories, and clinics. In addition, data input to the registry is limited because of the prohibition against mandatory HIV testing; thus it may not be sensitive to potential cases.

Local and international experts have been baffled by the low prevalence and slow growth of HIV/AIDS in the Philippines because the conditions that can make the situation explosive are present.

Two other possible reasons cited by the *HIV/AIDS Country Profile Philippines, 2002,* are the archipelagic nature of the country, which slows down the movement of people, and its detachment from mainland Asia, which may have helped shield it from the rapid cross-transfer of the epidemic.

HIV/AIDS Is a Low Priority

Because of this low prevalence, the general public and the bureaucracy tend to view the problem as a low priority. Consequently, funds are not allocated for HIV/AIDS and go instead toward supposedly more urgent purposes like schools, infrastructure, and livelihood opportunities. But the low figures can give a false sense of security, for behind such impressive numbers, health experts agree, may lie a danger that is hidden and growing. They warn that such figures may not last long because the current epidemiological picture shows evidence of high-risk situations and practices that could lead to a growing epidemic. These include, according to the NHSSS, a high rate of sexually transmitted infections (STIs), consistently low condom use rates among sex workers (less than 30%), the increasing practice of anal sex, the trend for people to become more sexually active at a younger age, and the sharing of needles among injecting drug users (IDUs). Thus the impressive statistics may represent the calm before the storm. There may be a "tsunami" of AIDS heading this way. Indeed, the Philippine National AIDS Council (PNAC) is convinced that for every case documented, the government is most likely missing three or four more cases. Jean-Marc Olivé, WHO representative to the Philippines, echoes that opinion and believes that the number of individuals in the Philippines already infected with HIV/AIDS is somewhere between 6,000 and 10,000. Many victims are unwilling to be tested; hence, data from the country's approximately 500 testing centers (comprised mainly of blood banks and testing centers for overseas workers) and ten sentinel sites covered by the NHSSS are reflective only of the vulnerable groups that have been willing to be tested and do not reveal the velocity of transmission. . . .

Populations Most Vulnerable to the Disease

In an interview for this study, Dr. Roderick Poblete, director of the PNAC, pointed to five groups that are most vulnerable to HIV infection—women, young adults, MSM [men who have sex with men], sex workers, and OFWs [overseas Filipino workers]. The characteristics of each group were described in the *HIV/AIDS Country Profile Philippines, 2002*, and this section paraphrases that description.

Women—Women tend to be vulnerable to HIV/AIDS as a result of various physiological, socioeconomic, and cultural circumstances. Women are less capable of protecting themselves or negotiating for safe sex—a factor that applies to female sex workers negotiating with clients as well as to women in general who may be put at risk by their partners' risky behavior. A 2001 study conducted in three major cities in the Philippines found that about 40% of women respondents lacked the confidence to ask their regular partners to use condoms even if they had adequate knowledge of HIV/AIDS and other STIs. About 43% of them admitted to having been forced into sex at times, and 15% believed it was their "obligation" to have sex with their partners.

More than 20% of all reported HIV cases in the Philippines involve male-to-male transmission.

Young Adults—The 3rd YAFS [Young Adult Fertility and Sexuality] study, conducted in 2002 by the University of the Philippines Population Institute, showed that young adults have liberal attitudes on sexuality and sexual practices. At the same time, unfortunately, they still seem to have poor knowledge about STIs and AIDS. One-third thought AIDS can be cured, and a large proportion thought that they were not vulnerable to the disease. This was confirmed by another study, conducted in 2000 among third- and fourth-year students

(18–22 years old) in Manila universities to identify their level of knowledge, attitudes, and perceptions about HIV/AIDS and other STIs. That study found that, despite better knowledge about transmission and prevention, misconceptions and risky behavior were still present. Premarital sex and inconsistent condom use were common. Condoms were used only during intercourse with sex workers (and even then, not consistently). The combination of immature sexual attitudes and lack of information places young adults at a risk of contracting HIV/AIDS, and efforts by conservative lobbies to stifle sex education in schools does not help in reducing the risk.

Men Who Have Sex with Men—More than 20% of all reported HIV cases in the Philippines involve male-to-male transmission. The actual rate, however, could be much higher since the stigma attached to homosexuality prevents many men from admitting that they have engaged in homosexual activity or from coming out to their families and work colleagues. Discrimination, harassment, and outright physical violence against homosexuals still occur in the Philippines. Moreover, religious attitudes labeling homosexual acts as "sinful" perpetuate the stigma. As a result of these conditions, many MSM live in the shadows, maintaining their anonymity by keeping sexual relationships casual and discreet. This very secretiveness, however, hinders access to HIV/AIDS information, education, and treatment, leaving MSM at a high risk of contracting HIV/AIDS.

Sex Workers—The illegal status of sex workers hinders their access to information on ... STIs, health services, and education programs, increasing their vulnerability to infection. Moreover, this makes them unable to negotiate for safe sex and impose safe sexual practices on their clients. A 2000 Health Action Information Network (HAIN) study titled "A Matter of Time" revealed different risk levels among various types of sex workers. Women and child sex workers were more susceptible to infection than males because of a lesser

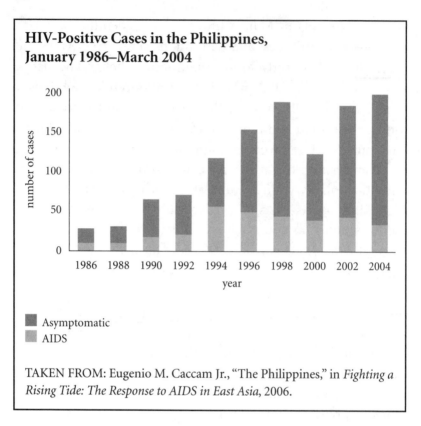

**HIV-Positive Cases in the Philippines,
January 1986–March 2004**

TAKEN FROM: Eugenio M. Caccam Jr., "The Philippines," in *Fighting a Rising Tide: The Response to AIDS in East Asia,* 2006.

ability to negotiate for safe sex. On the other hand, freelance sex workers and male sex workers were getting little information on HIV/AIDS because there were few information programs that targeted them.

The practice of issuing certificates to entertainment establishments that ensure clients of "wholesome" and "sanitary" services was questioned since sex workers and establishment owners may conceal risky behavior and infections to get their certification. Clients who perceive these places as being free of HIV/AIDS or STIs may be lulled into a false sense of security by these certificates and thus unwittingly engage in risky behavior.

Overseas Filipino Workers—Current statistics indicate that about 30% of Filipinos infected with HIV are OFWs. The vulnerability of migrant workers is determined and influenced by several factors, including limited knowledge about HIV/AIDS, low condom use, poor health-seeking behavior, and an attitude of invincibility toward HIV/AIDS. A gap between knowledge and behavior has also been reported. The everyday reality of their lives, such as emotional loneliness caused by being away from home, cultural adaptations, and difficult working conditions, also contributes to their vulnerability.

The lack of knowledge about HIV/AIDS among seafarers, combined with their high-risk sexual practices, put them at a particularly high risk of contracting HIV. About 20% of the 1.2 million seafarers worldwide are Filipino. In 1996, there were 307 shipping companies deploying 200,000 Filipino seamen. Macho values—including a belief that it is natural for them to "taste" women at every port—put seafarers at risk. Commercial sex workers (CSWs) are present in almost every port and are sometimes brought on board. But according to a study by the Department of Labor and Employment's Occupational Safety and Health Center, only 49% of seafarers practice safe sex.

With the increasing number of OFWs who are HIV-positive, serious attention should be given to protecting them and reducing their vulnerability. Social welfare institutions must be equipped to respond to the needs of those infected and to prevent infection among those who are about to leave. . . .

It is projected, however, that the danger of an epidemic remains.

Future Projections

For a country that registers a low incidence of HIV/AIDS, it is rather difficult, if not moot, to make projections five years hence, particularly if the purpose of the exercise is to change behavior, influence policy, or generate more resources. . . .

It is projected, however, that the danger of an epidemic remains since the ingredients are already present—e.g., increased sexual activity of the youth, an already large sex industry, the high rate of STIs both among the vulnerable groups and the general population, inadequate knowledge about the disease, poor health-seeking behavior, and a suspected increase in the number of IDUs. Added to this is the dwindling of resources given to combating the disease (because the "low and slow" spread of the disease tends to lessen the priority given to it in the authorities' and other people's minds). For that reason, the [Fourth] AIDS Medium Term Plan [AMTP] was drafted on the basis of this future potential for an epidemic. In order to maintain the low incidence of the disease, the plan seeks to do the following:

- intensify prevention interventions among highly vulnerable groups identified in AMTP III—CSWs, MSM, IDUs, and clients of CSWs—and scale up prevention efforts toward other vulnerable groups (e.g., OFWs, youth, and children)

- expand coverage and integrate HIV/AIDS in the development priorities at the local level, giving priority to identified risk zones

- improve the coverage and quality of care and support for PLWHA [persons living with HIV/AIDS]

- strengthen management support systems for the national response

A notable difference is that the current plan is more explicit than its predecessor with regard to attention to infected and affected children. Its policy directions also include mechanisms to ensure a protected level of funding support, the setting up of systems to measure the quality of every intervention, and the alignment of directions and goals with the Philippines Medium-Term Development Plan, the Millennium

Development Goals, the United Nations General Assembly Special Session on HIV/AIDS (UNGASS) Declaration of Commitment on HIV/AIDS, and the Association of Southeast Asian Nations (ASEAN) Joint Ministerial Statement and other international commitments. Specifically, the objectives of the new plan are fourfold: (1) to increase the proportion of the population with risk-free practices; (2) to increase the access of people infected and affected by HIV/AIDS to quality information, treatment, care, and support services; (3) to improve accepting attitudes toward people infected and affected by HIV/AIDS; and (4) to improve the efficiency and quality of management systems in support of HIV/AIDS programs and services. The third objective is particularly significant as there is now a more explicit statement about the need for an accepting attitude toward those infected and affected. . . .

The Philippines is fortunate—at least for the moment—to be a low-prevalence country. The prevalence and growth of the disease are described as low and slow, and its occurrence remains concentrated in five vulnerable groups. However, it is generally recognized—and feared—that there is a lurking danger, that the low-prevalence figures are just the tip of the iceberg, and that there might in fact be a "tsunami" of HIV/AIDS headed toward this country. Thus, the current favorable situation should not be a reason for complacency and laxity. Rather, both the general population and other stakeholders should continue to be vigilant and presume that for every case reported there might be more unreported. Only through vigilance can the country be assured that it can prevent and manage this epidemic, which greatly affects those who are among the most impoverished.

Pakistan Is on the Verge of an AIDS Epidemic

Mohammad A. Rai, Haider J. Warraich, Syed H. Ali, and Vivek R. Nerurkar

Mohammad A. Rai, Haider J. Warraich, and Syed H. Ali are professors in the biological and biomedical sciences at Aga Khan University in Pakistan; Vivek R. Nerurkar is a professor at the John A. Burns School of Medicine at the University of Honolulu. In the following viewpoint, they argue that Pakistan has avoided an AIDS epidemic for twenty years but that the disease is growing among high-risk groups like injecting drug users, sex workers, and truck drivers. They conclude that a strong government response is needed quickly if Pakistan is to avoid a full-blown epidemic.

As you read, consider the following questions:

1. According to the authors, the first reports of HIV in Pakistan occurred in what year and implicated what as the cause?

2. What are Hijras, and what is the prevalence of HIV among them in Karachi, according to the authors?

3. What do the authors say the private sector in Pakistan has done to combat AIDS?

Mohammad A. Rai, Haider J. Warraich, Syed H. Ali, and Vivek R. Nerurkar, "HIV/ AIDS in Pakistan: The Battle Begins," *Retrovirology*, March 21, 2007. Copyright © 2007 by Biomed Central Ltd. Reproduced by permission.

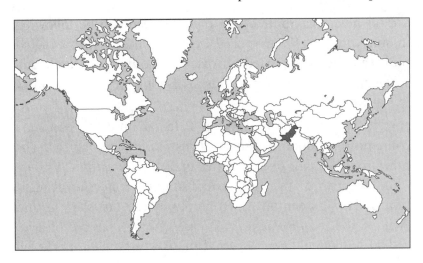

Abstract

Pakistan, the second most populous Muslim nation in the world, has started to finally experience and confront the HIV/AIDS epidemic. The country had been relatively safe from any indigenous HIV cases for around two decades, with most of the infections being attributable to deported HIV positive migrants from the Gulf States. However, the virus finally seems to have found a home-base, as evidenced by the recent HIV outbreaks among the injection drug user community. Extremely high-risk behavior has also been documented among Hijras (sex workers) and long-distance truck drivers. The weak government response coupled with the extremely distressing social demographics of this South-Asian republic also helps to compound the problem. The time is ripe now to prepare in advance, to take the appropriate measures to curtail further spread of the disease. If this opportunity is not utilized right now, little if at all could be done later.

Introduction

Pakistan, the world's second most populous Muslim nation, has started to finally experience and confront the HIV/AIDS epidemic. Largely portrayed as having [been] free of this menace till now, this South-Asian republic seems to be following in suit with its HIV-havocked neighbor, India. With isolated outbreaks being reported all over the country, time already seems to be running out for the sixth most populous country in the world.

The first reports of HIV in Pakistan in 1987 implicate contaminated blood transfusions[1] as one of the culprits. The other route alludes to expatriates or Pakistanis settled abroad. These seem to be the more important risk factor for acquisition of HIV, as demonstrated amply by the fact that around 70% of the total positive HIV cases from a sample of over 15,000 individuals over a period of six years (1986–1992) fell into this category.[2] The bulk of the infected were deported workers from the Gulf States.[3] Pakistan, as compared to its neighbors, has remained relatively safe from any indigenously acquired cases of HIV for about two decades. The situation, however, changed in 2004 when Pakistan experienced its first full-fledged HIV outbreak.[4] In the remote desert town of Larkana, the HIV bubble-burst took place amongst the injecting drug user (IDU) community. What this basically meant was that the virus had finally found a home-base, as evidenced later by outbreaks all over the nation.[5]

High-Risk Populations

The HIV/AIDS epidemic in Pakistan is following along the same atypical lines as it has done so far in the rest of Asia. Starting from isolated high-risk population subgroups, the virus jumps the barrier to cross into the mainstream general populace. Once this barrier is crossed, little if at all anything can be done to prevent a complete HIV onslaught.

Similar to its south-east Asian neighbors, the greatest risk for the spread of HIV in Pakistan stems from IDU. Currently estimated at over 180,000 in number,[6] the ongoing strife in Afghanistan, the world's largest poppy-producing country, seems only to swell up this number even more in the future.[7]

IDU all over the country have started recording alarmingly high rates of HIV. According to the latest figures released by the National AIDS Control Program of Pakistan, HIV/AIDS prevalence among IDUs has jumped from 0.4% in December 2003 to 7.6% in 2004. However, in Larkana, where Pakistan's first HIV outbreak among IDU was reported, the number approached an astounding twenty-seven percent.[4] After the Larkana episode, HIV has been documented among IDU all over Pakistan. Currently, IDU do not comprise the bulk of drug users in Pakistan.[8] The number of IDU is bound to increase in the near future, and as this happens, the relative cases of HIV/AIDS will also rise. The first hurdle in the spread of HIV seems to be already traversed.

Sex workers in Pakistan represent the second most serious threat for HIV transmission. The government refuses to accept illicit sex underway in the country, although there are established prostitution centers in all the major cities of Pakistan. The so-called 'red-light' areas, in addition to female prostitutes, also house Hijras—male transvestites. These Hijras provide valuable insight into HIV demographics, as data pertaining to female commercial sex workers is very limited. Reports[5] suggest that the HIV prevalence among Hijras in Karachi, a city of 13 million people in southern Pakistan, approximates around 4%. The situation is bound to be even worse in the rural parts, particularly in the Pathan-dominated northern Pakistan, where homosexuality is socially tolerated.[9] The majority of men having sex with men in Pakistan are married,[10] which brings into light their possible potential as acting as a bridge to the general population.

Similar to its south-east Asian neighbors, the greatest risk for the spread of HIV in Pakistan stems from IDU.

Truck drivers are also a very important subgroup, primarily because of their role in fuelling the HIV epidemic in neighboring Madras, India.[11] In a survey done in Lahore, Pakistan's central hub for long-distance truckers, over 49% of them reported having sex with another man.[12] The possibility of horizontal ellipsis across the border from India has also been raised.[13]

Once the high-risk populations have acquired the virus, it is only a matter of time before the general populace falls prey to it. IDU, commercial sex workers, truck drivers, etc., facilitate in bridging this gap. What is alarming is the fact that once the virus moves from the urban population to the rural population, the effect will be much more catastrophic, not only because the bulk of the Pakistani population resides here (only 34% lives in urban areas)[17] but also due to almost non-existent health care facilities.

HIV is considered extremely shameful, particularly in the rural setting.

Steps Underway

Decades of corruption and poor planning of resources have translated into a fight for Pakistan's very own continued existence. Keeping this in mind and the horde of other problems currently encountering Pakistan, any efforts directed towards prevention and control of HIV/AIDS are quite laudable.

The bulk of the credit in this regard goes to the private sector. Over 50 non-governmental organizations (NGO) are working to improve the HIV/AIDS status quo in Pakistan.[5] Their work ranges from providing needle-exchange programs for IDU to spreading awareness about HIV/AIDS to the masses. Worth mentioning is the organization, 'AMAL,' which means 'action' in Pakistan's national language, Urdu. It has outreach HIV training programs focusing not only on IDU but also for the out-of-the-limelight population, female sex workers.

Recommended Anti-HIV Programmes for Pakistan

Needle and syringe exchange programmes for injecting drug users. These programmes are technically and administratively simple, address a widely acknowledged problem and face no strong opposition. Programmes are delivered through contracted NGOs [nongovernmental organizations]. Successful harm reduction interventions are already provided in some cities by NGOs, but scaling up will present challenges.

Ministries other than the MOH [Ministry of Health] will need to be engaged with, and ideally local ex-user champions can be found to act as advocates. NGO staff will need to develop trust with law-enforcement agencies and local community leaders.

Comprehensive sexual health care for male and transgender sex workers. Although the mathematical model suggests that male, and particularly transgender, sex workers will play a central role in the future of the HIV epidemic in Pakistan, informants believed that provision of effective interventions for them—e.g. distribution of condoms and lubricants, treatment of STIs [sexually transmitted infections], voluntary testing and counseling for HIV—will be far from straightforward.

Interventions for MTSW [male transvestite sex workers] are likely to have least resonance with society of the five interventions we propose, will be difficult to explain to the public, and will likely face opposition from powerful groups and individuals. MTSW are not organised politically to demand recognition or services. As yet, no prominent champion has emerged to raise awareness.

Programme for Research and Capacity Building in Sexual and Reproductive Health and HIV in Developing Countries, "HIV in Pakistan," April 2009. www.aidslex.org.

On the other side, the current government policy falls under the auspices of the National HIV/AIDS Strategic Framework. The program has four foci: improved HIV prevention, expanding interventions among vulnerable groups, preventing transfusion-related infections and improving infrastructure.[15] With over Rs. [rupee] 2.9 billion (US $48 million) at its disposal, the program hopefully would chalk out a practical, concrete plan and then initiate work to implement it.

The Social Demographics

It may sound ludicrous, but the fact remains that to properly combat any problem, the affected have to first accept it and then conquer over it. The society in Pakistan has as yet not accepted HIV/AIDS as having anything to do with them. Trends may be changing, but the age-old stigmas and taboos related to HIV still persist. HIV is considered extremely shameful, particularly in the rural setting. Even discussions on this topic are frowned upon. Awareness about HIV/AIDS in general is extremely limited. The severity of the situation could be deduced from a survey conducted among schoolteachers in the capital city, Islamabad. An outstanding sixty percent of the teachers responded by saying that 'they thought HIV was irrelevant in our cultural setting.'[16] This awareness and acceptance issue would indeed be a big challenge, because 'teachers' as well as 'children' will need to be taught.

UNAIDS' latest figures estimate the number of cases in Pakistan bordering 85,000.[14] Underreporting and limited surveillance means that the actual number of infected is much higher. Keeping in mind the poor health care facilities, the appallingly low literacy rate (in 2001, the illiteracy rate for Pakistani women over 15 years old was 72%),[17] and a mushrooming population (growth rate of Pakistan lies at 2.5%),[17] the stakes for a battle against HIV are indeed very [high].

Conclusion

The situation concerning Pakistan and HIV is indeed very precarious. The country lies at a very crucial junction. HIV has as yet not exploded. Most of the populace remains safe, for now. However, concentrated epidemics have emerged, which means that very little time is left before a steep rise in infections occurs. The battle against HIV/AIDS in Pakistan has to be fought on a number of fronts: not just the afflicted population, but also on changing people's perspectives and ushering in the proper government policies and response measures. Neighboring China serves as a good example to follow as regards formulation of a national policy about HIV/AIDS.[18] The government has to come forward and face the truth about HIV in Pakistan. Embarking not only upon national-level mass awareness programs, practical steps including widespread screening for the high-risk populations has also to be instituted. Stigma and discrimination about HIV/AIDS in society could only be removed when prominent figures including politicians and sports stars start discussing HIV/AIDS in public. As soon as this stigmatization barrier is overcome, a major chunk of the battle against HIV in Pakistan would be conquered. What has to be reiterated is that the time to act is now. Timely steps taken at the present can go a long way in preventing a widespread HIV epidemic in Pakistan.

References

1. Khanani RM, Hafeez A, Rab SM, Rasheed S: "Human immunodeficiency virus-associated disorders in Pakistan." *AIDS Res Hum Retroviruses* 1988, 4 (2): 149-54.

2. N Sheikh A, Khan A, Mithani C, Khurshid M: "A view of HIV-I infection in Karachi." *J Pak Med Assoc* 1994, 44 (1): 8-11.

3. Shah SA, Khan OA, Kristensen S, Vermund SH: "HIV-infected workers deported from the Gulf States: impact on Southern Pakistan." *Int J STD AIDS* 1999, 10 (12): 812-4.

4. Shah SA, Altaf A, Mujeeb SA, Memon A: "An outbreak of HIV infection among injection drug users in a small town in Pakistan: potential for national implications." *Int J STD AIDS* 2004, 15 (3): 209.

5. *World Bank Report* [http://siteresources.worldbank.org/INTSAREGTOPHIVAIDS/Resources/HIV-AIDS-brief-August06-PKA.pdf] Updated: Apr 4, 2006, Accessed: May 8, 2006.

6. Deany P: *HIV and Injecting Drug Use: A New Challenge to Sustainable Human Development 2000.* [http://www.undp.org/hiv/publications/deany.htm] *UNDP HIV and Development Programme.* Accessed: May 2, 2006.

7. Strathdee SA, Zafar T, Brahmbhatt H, Baksh A, ul Hassan S: "Rise in needle sharing among injection drug users in Pakistan during the Afghanistan war." *Drug Alcohol Depend* 71 (1): 17-24. 2003, Jul 20.

8. *Pakistan: Country Profile. United Nations Office on Drugs and Crime* [http://www.unodc.org/pakistan/en/country_profile.html] Accessed: 8 May 2006.

9. Hanif M: "No safer sex for Pakistan's gays." In *World AIDS*. Volume 11. London: Panos Institute; 1993.

10. Khan OA, Hyder AA: "HIV/AIDS among men who have sex with men in Pakistan." *Sex Health Exch* 1998, 5 (2): 12-3.

11. Shreedhar J: "AIDS in India." *Harv AIDS Rev* 1995, Fall: 2-9.

12. Agha S: "Potential for HIV transmission among truck drivers in Pakistan." *Aids* 14 (15): 2404-6. 2000 Oct 20.

13. Rai MA, Khan MN, Khan S, Khanani R, Ali SH: "Pakistan/India open borders ... to HIV?" *AIDS* 20 (4): 634-5. 2006 Feb 28.

14. UNAIDS: *Report on the Global AIDS Epidemic 2006.* [http://www.unaids.org/en/HIV_data/2006GlobalReport/default.asp] Accessed: 2 Feb 2007.

15. *Pakistan Millenium Development Goals Report* [http://www.un.org.pk/undp/publication/PMDGR05.pdf] 2005. Accessed: May 11, 2006.

16. Shaikh IA, Shaikh MA: "Teachers attitudes about HIV/AIDS prevention education in secondary schools." *J Coll Physicians Surg Pak* 2005, 15 (9): 582.

17. UNAIDS, UNICEF, WHO: *Epidemiological fact sheet, 2004.* [http://data.unaids.org/Publications/Fact-Sheets01/pakistan_EN.pdf] 2004. Update: Pakistan. Accessed: 21 Sept 2006.

18. Shao Y: "AIDS epidemic at age 25 and control efforts in China." *Retrovirology* 3: 87. 2006 Dec 1.

The HIV/AIDS Epidemic Creates Orphans in China and Worldwide

César Chelala

César Chelala is an international public health consultant and the author of AIDS: A Modern Epidemic. *In the following viewpoint, he notes that AIDS epidemics in China and Asia are creating a growing number of orphans. He notes that the number of orphans will continue to increase for many years even in countries where rates of HIV are falling. He argues that China needs to undertake a major educational campaign to prevent the spread of AIDS and to reduce the stigmatization of AIDS orphans. He also calls for more resources to be devoted to the needs of AIDS orphans.*

As you read, consider the following questions:

1. How many children will be orphaned by 2010, according to Chelala, and how many of them will be orphaned by AIDS?

2. What health problems are children orphaned because of their parents' deaths by AIDS likely to face, according to Chelala?

3. Based on a 2004 survey, what percentage of rural residents in China had heard of HIV/AIDS?

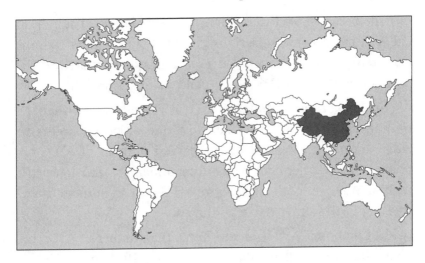

The rapid spread of the HIV infection in China is having a devastating impact on the country's children, and threatens to become an epidemic with significant social and public health repercussions due to the rapid rise in [the] AIDS orphan population. The increased number of AIDS orphans in China parallels the increasing number of AIDS orphans worldwide, and is one of the most serious consequences of the AIDS epidemic today.

> *Although proportionally the number of AIDS orphans in Asia is much lower than in sub-Saharan Africa, in absolute numbers there are more orphans due to AIDS in Asia than in Africa.*

The Problem Is Worsening

In rural China, many villages that up to now have had very few orphans have seen their rates soar following AIDS deaths of the parents as a result of blood transfusions with contaminated needles. Until recently the remaining relatives used to take care of the children. Because in many cases those relatives are now affected by HIV/AIDS, they have become unable to provide basic support to children in their families. The toll on children has become so serious that UNICEF [United Nations Children's Fund] has included new indicator[s] related to the prevalence of HIV/AIDS in its "child risk measure."

In 2003 it was estimated that worldwide more than 13 million children under 15 had lost one or both parents to AIDS. Although Thailand has the largest number of AIDS orphans—usually defined as children under 15 who have lost their mother or both parents to AIDS—their number is increasing fast in other Asian countries.

In Cambodia, Malaysia and India, the number of AIDS orphans has increased by 400 percent from 1994 to 1997. This rate of increase is similar to that of countries such as Namibia, South Africa and Botswana. Although proportionally the number of AIDS orphans in Asia is much lower than in sub-Saharan Africa, in absolute numbers there are more orphans due to AIDS in Asia than in Africa.

The majority of people in China still don't know how HIV is transmitted.

Orphaning is a worldwide problem. It is estimated that by 2010, 106 million children will lose one or both parents, and 25 million of them will be orphaned because of AIDS. According to estimates of China's Ministry of Health, there are at least 100,000 AIDS orphans in China. UNICEF's China Office estimates that over the next five years 150,000 to 250,000 additional children will be orphaned by AIDS.

Since 2003, UNICEF has worked with local health authorities and workers, the Women's Federation and communities to provide both psychological and social support to children affected by AIDS. It has also provided support to Summer Camps for Children Affected by AIDS, helping raise awareness about their needs.

Children orphaned because of their parents' deaths by AIDS are likely to be malnourished and unschooled, and are at greater risk of becoming HIV-infected themselves. At the same time, because they are emotionally vulnerable, when they grow up they may tend to engage in risky sexual behavior that may lead to a vicious cycle of abuse and exploitation.

The Number of Orphans
Will Continue to Rise

What makes this situation particularly worrisome is that the number of orphans will continue to rise for at least the next decade. That is why, even in a country where HIV prevalence has declined, the number of orphans will continue to be high. According to Dr. Peter Piot, executive director of UNAIDS [Joint United Nations Programme on HIV/AIDS], "The orphan crisis is a major reason for introducing treatment for adults on a wider scale."

Orphans due to HIV/AIDS are part of a much larger problem, since countries that have high rates of AIDS orphans also have [a] high number of children directly affected by the epidemic, and who are often just as vulnerable. Although their total number is difficult to assess, it has been estimated that over 3 million children worldwide are living with HIV/AIDS.

It is necessary to develop a major educational campaign to make people aware of the dangers of the infection not only to them but also the risks it poses to their children. The majority of people in China still don't know how HIV is transmitted. According to a survey carried out in 2004 by the Futures Group Europe and the Beijing-based Horizon Research Group, only 8.7 [percent] of Chinese knew how HIV is transmitted and 25 percent of rural residents hadn't even heard of the infection.

To help AIDS orphans in a more immediate and practical way it is necessary to strengthen the capacity of extended families to protect and care for orphan[ed] children by providing them with financial aid by local councils or provincial governments. Orphan[ed] children's special needs should also be addressed through community-based responses and by increasing the capacity of local orphanages.

It is also important to support the work of nongovernmental organizations (NGOs) such as the China AIDS Orphan Fund [that] have been working in collaboration with other NGOs to improve Chinese orphans' health, education, and quality of life.

It is important to diminish the stigma surrounding the HIV infection. Often times, children who have lost their parents to AIDS are assumed to be also infected with HIV, which further stigmatizes them. It is critical to develop new government policies including legal, education and labor frameworks, and to make sure that these policies will be followed.

Periodical and Internet Sources Bibliography

The following articles have been selected to supplement the diverse views presented in this chapter.

AVERT	"AIDS Orphans." www.avert.org.
AVERT	"The Origin of AIDS and HIV and the First Cases of AIDS." www.avert.org.
CSR Asia	"Philippines Faces Up to AIDS Crisis," February 8, 2006. www.csr-asia.com.
Paul Drain	"Africa's Devastating Challenge: HIV/AIDS and Extreme Poverty," *SeattlePi*, August 6, 2006.
Economist	"AIDS: DARC Continent," July 17, 2008.
Economist	"AIDS in China: Blood Debts," January 18, 2007.
IRIN	"Egypt: New Report Warns of HIV Epidemic," December 30, 2009.
IRIN	"HIV/AIDS: New HIV Report Turns Up Some Surprises," June 30, 2010.
Mamadou Mika Lom	"Senegal's Recipe for Success," *Africa Recovery*, June 2001.
Seth Mydans	"Low Rate of AIDS Virus in Philippines Is a Puzzle," *New York Times*, April 20, 2003.
Gabriel Rotello	"Andrew Sullivan Declares the 'End of AIDS'—Again," *Huffington Post*, June 25, 2007.
Andrew Sullivan	"1996: The Plague Ends," *Stranger* (Seattle), June 21, 2007.
Hilary White	"Philippine AIDS Rate Has Doubled with Increase of Condom Use," LifeSiteNews.com, February 3, 2006. www.lifesitenews.com.

GLOBALVIEWPOINTS

CHAPTER 2

Treatment of HIV/AIDS

In Sub-Saharan Africa, Failure to Accept Scientific Consensus Interferes with HIV Treatment

Marco Evers

Marco Evers works as a journalist for the science and technology section of Spiegel Online, *the English-language international edition of the weekly German newsmagazine* der Spiegel. *In the following viewpoint, he reports that in many African nations, anti-AIDS efforts are hampered by superstition and ignorance. He points, for example, to Gambia, where the president claims to be able to cure AIDS with a special concoction of herbs, and to South Africa, where a government minister claimed that showering would prevent HIV transmission. Evers notes AIDS treatment is improving, but delivering that treatment is complicated in Africa by poor health care and education.*

As you read, consider the following questions:

1. Who is Fadzai Gwaradzimba and what does Evers say happened to her?
2. How has life expectancy in Botswana changed in the last twenty-five years, according to the author?
3. What does Evers say is the only positive piece of news about AIDS in Africa?

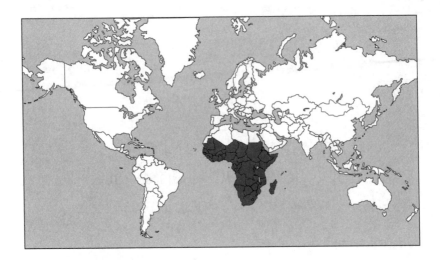

It's a story, set in the tiny, Western African country of Gambia, that would almost be funny—if it weren't so outrageous and tragic.

Miracle Cures

The country, clinging to the banks of the Gambia River as it winds toward the coast, is ruled by 41-year-old Yahya Jammeh, an autocrat who has a thing for white garb. And he aims high—he has resolved to transform his country into an African version of the rich, Asian city-state Singapore by 2020. Quite a goal for a country of 1.6 million with a low literacy rate and 75 percent of the population living off the land. But compared to Jammeh's most recent vision, reinventing Gambia as a center of trade and finance sounds almost plausible.

Jammeh—a military officer who staged a successful putsch [coup] in 1994—is not just the president. He's also a healer on a divine mission. In January of this year [2007], he summoned a number of his acolytes together with foreign diplomats and revealed to them that he had made an extraordinary discovery. He announced that, in addition to asthma, he was now capable of healing Acquired Immune Deficiency Syndrome (AIDS)—the epidemic that ravages sub-Saharan Africa like no other region of the world. More than 15 million Africans have already died of AIDS, and a further 25 million are infected with the HIV virus which causes the disease.

On Thursdays—Jammeh's healing powers are only available to him on that day of the week, he says—the president frequently allows Gambian television to film him as he defeats AIDS: Patients lie flat on their backs as the president whirls around them and mumbles verses from the Koran. He slaps green sludge onto their skin, sprinkles liquid from an old Evian bottle over them and gives them a brown broth to drink. A quick banana snack completes the therapy.

He announced that, in addition to asthma, he was now capable of healing Acquired Immune Deficiency Syndrome.

That's it. Thanks to the power of the Koran and seven secret herbs this treatment, repeated over the course of several weeks, leads to the patient being cured of the lethal virus "with absolute certainty," as Jammeh says. But two requirements need to be met for it all to work. First: His patients have to renounce alcohol, tea, coffee and sex for the duration of their treatment—as well as theft. And second: Whoever is taking anti-viral medication has to stop doing so immediately, according to Jammeh.

Even more disturbing is that the Gambian minister of health supports his president—despite being a trained gynecologist educated in Ukraine and Ireland. The country's other institutions, including the Parliament, are doing the same. And on the streets of the Gambia, demonstrations can sometimes be seen—not against Jammeh, but in support of him.

The Disease of Shame

So far, one of the few within Gambia to voice any criticism has been the United Nations spokesperson there, Fadzai

Gwaradzimba. She said there was no proof for the success of Jammeh's method and that no one should believe they would no longer be infected following treatment by the president. Jammeh was so enraged that he immediately declared the UN representative unwelcome and forced her to leave the country within 48 hours.

Earlier, two high-ranking AIDS educators had already announced their resignation in the capital city of Banjul. They explained that, in light of Jammeh's healing mania, it was impossible to teach the population about the dangers of HIV and AIDS. Meanwhile Jammeh continues to up the ante. In early April [2007] he announced he has now acquired the ability to heal diabetes, and that—just as with asthma—he needs only five minutes to do so. Not all his subjects believe him—but quite a few do.

Abysmal governments and spooky despots: just two of the many reasons why HIV can rage almost unchecked south of the Sahara. Only a handful of African states have adopted a rational approach to AIDS. Senegal, Ghana and especially Uganda have achieved impressive results in their struggle against the spread of the virus. But in other African societies conditions often prevail that actually help HIV spread—even now, 25 years after the discovery of the lethal disease.

Everything is connected: superstition, illiteracy, poverty, disinformation, isolation, corruption, migration, prostitution, promiscuity, polygamy—and, of course, the silence. Even though AIDS represents a grade-A catastrophe in many parts of sub-Saharan Africa, the issue has remained taboo. No one speaks about it, no one confesses to being affected by it— neither those infected nor their relatives, neither religious leaders nor politicians.

Those who know they are infected prefer to claim they're not suffering from AIDS but only from the plethora of diseases that take hold thanks to the weakening of the immune system—tumors, for example, tuberculosis or pneumonia.

Some even claim to have been bewitched. Everything is better than AIDS, since AIDS is still considered the disease of shame.

The eldest son of former South African President Nelson Mandela died of the effects of AIDS at age 54, in early 2005. His father made the affliction public and urged his compatriots to finally speak openly about the epidemic—to no avail. In many parts of Africa, those who admit to being HIV-positive must fear being ostracized along with their relatives. Some have even been killed by angry neighbors after making their HIV-positive status public.

Everything is better than AIDS, since AIDS is still considered the disease of shame.

Persistent Legends

It's bizarre how so many countries succeed in denying an epidemic that sends masses of young people to the grave and hollows out entire societies from within. Farmers afflicted with AIDS are too weak to work in the fields. Teachers no longer teach. Soldiers die. Truck drivers, engineers, doctors and ministers, their wives and their children—they are all affected. AIDS is costing many countries all the economic progress made during the last 25 years.

Some companies routinely hire two applicants for a job opening because they know very well that soon only one of them will be left. Burials have become the most frequent family occasions in many regions. Twenty-five years ago, life expectancy in Botswana was still above 60. Now it has sunk to little more than 40. Twelve million children have become orphans due to AIDS. Many of them were infected with the virus before they were born or from their mother's milk.

Hardly any of these countries has even a semi-functional health system. Scientifically trained medical practitioners are rare and most of the ill seldom come into contact with them,

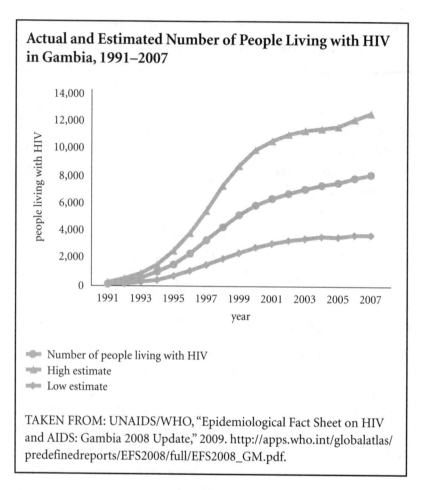

Actual and Estimated Number of People Living with HIV in Gambia, 1991–2007

Number of people living with HIV
High estimate
Low estimate

TAKEN FROM: UNAIDS/WHO, "Epidemiological Fact Sheet on HIV and AIDS: Gambia 2008 Update," 2009. http://apps.who.int/globalatlas/predefinedreports/EFS2008/full/EFS2008_GM.pdf.

if at all. Doctors can only estimate the overall infection rate, for example, by means of testing those they do come into contact with—pregnant women for example. And what they've found is breathtaking even for pessimistic experts. Every fifth person in Zambia, every fourth person in Namibia and every third birth in Zimbabwe and Botswana [are] HIV positive. With the exception of India, the absolute number of people with HIV is nowhere higher than in South Africa. The figure is above 6 million. More than a thousand South Africans die of AIDS every day.

Africans still go to their highly respected traditional healers for medical aid, healers that follow the tradition of their forefathers by tackling all ills with herbs and magic. In the best possible scenario, these healers could help solve the AIDS problem, and in many countries aid organizations are trying to recruit them for necessary educational work. But often the messages spread by such healers are part of the problem. In southern Africa, for example, millions of men are convinced an HIV infection can easily be cured—by means of sex with a virgin.

That condoms offer protection is far from common knowledge, and many of those who have heard don't believe it. Some believe condoms are irreconcilable with masculinity or even take them to be a conspiracy by white men aimed at lowering the African birth rate. Many also believe that condoms are infected with HIV by the West to reduce the African population. Many tribal leaders and traditional healers warn against the use of condoms—as does the Catholic Church. Under such circumstances, messages of prevention are often ignored.

That condoms offer protection is far from common knowledge, and many of those who have heard don't believe it.

Tragically, the HIV virus strikes people who are especially predisposed to it in Africa. Other venereal diseases such as syphilis, herpes [and] gonorrhea are also still widespread in the region—and they tend to make those who suffer from them more susceptible to the AIDS virus.

In addition, many women in sub-Saharan Africa have for generations been engaging in sexual practices that dramatically increase their own risk of infection. Before having sex, they use herbs, powder or cloths to remove all moisture from their vaginas. Men supposedly appreciate this practice because it makes the vagina dry, hot and tight. But so-called "dry sex" often leads to minor injuries to the mucous membrane, which facilitates HIV infection. AIDS educators are trying to encourage women [to] abandon this custom, but with only limited success.

South Africa

In theory, South Africa is the country that should be best equipped, in terms of economic power and infrastructure, to fight the epidemic. But South African politicians seem to be doing all they can to help the virus spread. They may not be quite as flamboyant as Gambia's presidential virus slayer, but they come close to being as dangerous. Thabo Mbeki, Mandela's successor as president, has repeatedly flirted with the long discredited ideas of the "AIDS dissidents," according to whom, AIDS is not caused by a virus, but by poverty and malnutrition.

Mbeki's former vice president, Jacob Zuma, has had unprotected sex with a woman who was HIV positive at the time. There was hardly any risk of infection, Zuma said publicly, since he showered immediately after having sex. It's astonishing that Zuma isn't more knowledgeable about the spread of HIV; he was, after all, previously the director of a national AIDS organization.

South African politicians seem to be doing all they can to help the virus spread.

And the South African minister of health, a med-school graduate, advises those infected not to take anti-viral medication in favor of a mixture of garlic, lemon, potatoes and red beet. That's better, she says, because the side effects are less severe. "Dr. Red Beet," as she is mockingly called, also sympathizes with German miracle healer Matthias Rath, who sells vitamin drinks in South Africa as an alleged alternative to established HIV medication.

In wealthier nations, AIDS has long ceased leading inevitably to death. The disease may not be curable, but modern medication can battle the viruses so effectively that it can no longer be detected in the blood. For a long time, however, the therapy was so expensive that only some 100,000 Africans benefited from it in 2003.

But things have changed—and this is the only positive piece of news about AIDS in Africa. Many countries and organizations provide billions of dollars to purchase medication at drastically reduced prices. Last year, about 1.3 million AIDS victims in sub-Saharan Africa had access to the medication they need to survive for the first time.

In other words, almost a third of those in need already receive help. By 2010, the UN [United Nations] wants to ensure that every afflicted person receives treatment.

The end of the epidemic could be near for African HIV patients. But the hurdles remain high: For the afflicted to be cured, their blood first needs to be examined by qualified personnel—of which there is a considerable lack. Hardly 10 percent of the population have taken an AIDS test in the most severely affected African countries.

The others often don't even know that such a thing exists.

In India, the Scientific Consensus Has Not Led to Effective HIV Treatment

Rupa Chinai

Rupa Chinai is an independent journalist based in Mumbai, India. In the following viewpoint, she argues that mainstream AIDS organizations have presented a misleading view of the disease. She says that HIV is not automatically a death sentence and that it is not solely reliant on sexual transmission. Rather, she argues that poverty and poor nutrition make people vulnerable to AIDS. She argues that AIDS organizations should focus less on distributing condoms and antiretroviral drugs and should instead concentrate on alleviating poverty and making sure those with HIV have access to fresh fruits and vegetables.

As you read, consider the following questions:

1. The AIDS widows Chinai talked to said that their husbands did not die because of AIDS but because of what other factors?

2. How many HIV patients did the Salvation Army follow in Mumbai; how many died within the course of a decade, according to the author?

3. Chinai says antiretroviral drugs are not a good solution to AIDS for what reasons?

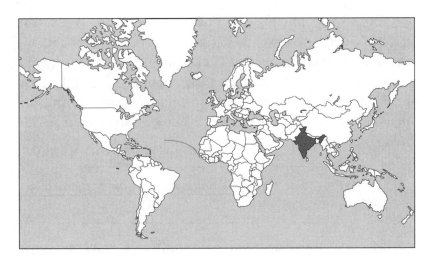

During the course of the past decade, women diagnosed as HIV/AIDS patients in Mumbai have been trying to say something important that deserves close attention. These widows, whose husbands died from AIDS, claim their experience is quite contrary to Western science, which insists that HIV is a "death sentence."

AIDS Is Not the Culprit

These AIDS widows have become "long-term survivors." For more than 12 to 14 years, they have been living well and have not felt the need to start antiretroviral (ARV) [drug] therapy. It was through good counseling groups that they found hope. They got access to good doctors whose detailed and regular check-ups caught infections early. They also found a support group among women with similar afflictions. Thereafter, a "positive attitude" became the buzzword in their lives.

These women share their firsthand experiences of this disease. They believe that their husbands did not suffer an early demise because of AIDS. They say their men died because of addiction to alcohol, *gutka* (chewing tobacco) or cigarettes, coupled with a careless attitude towards medication and failing to adopt changes in their lifestyle.

They extend this logic to their own situation. When first detected as HIV-positive, their vulnerability to cold, cough, fever and diarrhea increased. They also suffered from weight loss. These women believe that their physical vulnerability was more an outcome of their tension, fatigue after caring for their sick husbands and economic burden rather than AIDS-induced infections.

They believe that their husbands did not suffer an early demise because of AIDS.

Lata, who was diagnosed HIV-positive 14 years ago, says, "Coming to terms with our HIV status took us two to four years. We needed time to work out the anger we felt towards our husbands, the rejection of our families and to think quietly about how to deal with the fear."

Lata and other women have learned in the past decade that it is important to take care of their health. Sharda, another member of the group, says that she does not eat out and carries her own drinking water wherever she goes. This has greatly helped in reducing bouts of diarrhea, cold, cough and fever. The group members are no longer careless about medication and do not sit home alone and mope. If they cannot find paid work, they volunteer to help other AIDS patients.

"What kills people is the lack of hope, tension, the absence of family and social support and our economic plight. With all other illnesses, even TB [tuberculosis, an infection of the lungs] or cancer, everyone wants to help. HIV makes everyone turn away. At this time, if you find even one person who can help you stand on your own feet, you have a chance," says Sharda.

Fighting AIDS with Diet

Their diet primarily consists of *dal* (lentils) and rice. Seasonal fruits and green vegetables that they desperately need are a rare luxury but they are learning that food that is cheap, seasonal and locally available is a powerhouse of energy that can boost the body's immune system in fighting AIDS-related opportunistic infections. A daily diet consisting of a banana, some lemons and a couple of dates, along with seasonal fruits and vegetables like gourd, is adequate.

The mega bucks spent in the name of AIDS have not reached them. Attending tailoring classes and receiving support in finding work is helping these widows to start taking charge of their lives. Some key issues that would make a difference in the care and support of the AIDS afflicted, they say, is ensuring access to TB treatment along with nutrition support for those on therapy; the presence of well-trained doctors in rural areas; security for their children and organizational support in solving legal and other disputes with family members.

This phenomenon, taking place within the general population in Mumbai, is important to monitor. Several support groups for AIDS patients pioneered this approach and noted a regression of the disease. It also found some important clues to why HIV-positive patients progress into disease.

Fixated on the sexual transmission theory of HIV/AIDS, mainstream Western science has resisted such evidence and held fast to the view that the answer to AIDS lies in condoms, sex education and ARVs alone.

Following a cohort of 900 HIV patients from within the general population in Mumbai, the Salvation Army for instance, found that only 15 had died in the course of a decade. The main causes of death were TB or malnutrition, often coupled with alcohol abuse amongst the men. Such evidence calls for broad-based interventions, through policies that focus on access to real nutrition (as opposed to chemical-based

Nutrition and AIDS in Africa

Health historians say that AIDS in Africa is a consequence of the depletion of the body's nutrition pool down through the generations and the destruction of the immune system. As sub-Saharan Africa plunged deeper into the cycle of poverty, malnutrition and civil war, it also suffered epidemics of Ebola and Marburg [viruses] or Lassa fever, . . . AIDS could be the result of this depletion of the nutrition pool.

Rupa Chinai, "HIV/AIDS in India:
Rampant Misdiagnosis and the Burden of the Disease,"
The WIP, December 4, 2008. http://thewip.net.

supplements) and comprehensive primary health services, which include addiction treatment.

This implies the need to take a hard look at our trade and development policies (which have caused the loss of local food self-sufficiency) and our narrow approach to health issues through "vertical programs"—all of which are leading to adverse health outcomes.

Fixated on the sexual transmission theory of HIV/AIDS, mainstream Western science has resisted such evidence and held fast to the view that the answer to AIDS lies in condoms, sex education and ARVs alone. The public messages, communicated at great financial expense, insist that HIV/AIDS spreads through multi-partner sexual activity and bodily fluids, and knows no barriers of class or social status.

AIDS Attacks the Marginalized

Now the wheel has turned full circle and the AIDS lobby is steadily backtracking on its earlier pronouncements. Forced to come down on its earlier inflated estimates of the numbers affected by HIV/AIDS, it now admits that AIDS assails only the marginalized and specific segments of the population.

This reversal is evident in a new report by the Commission on AIDS in Asia, tabled with the UN [United Nations] in March 2008. It states that the epidemic is restricted to specific and vulnerable groups engaged in "high-risk" activities. Such people, says the report, are those who engage in unprotected paid sex (commercial sex work), injecting drug users who share contaminated needles and syringes, and men who have unprotected sex with other men (MSM).

This assertion of the Asia Commission appears to be correct and conforms to the trend noted in cities like Mumbai during the course of two decades. Here, the reality on the ground has clearly shown that those who suffer a rapid downslide into AIDS and death are primarily those from the low socio-economic group. Commercial sex workers, injecting drug users, homosexual men and alcoholics appear to be more vulnerable.

These drugs do not offer a cure and they are expensive to sustain on a lifelong basis, even when it is the cheaper, generic version.

The intense pressure of drug companies to launch patients into ARV treatment is, meanwhile, not without problems. Evidence from Mumbai's government-run J.J. Hospital reveals that the drug is helping patients whose CD4 count [CD4 cells are a type of white blood cell that fights infection] falls below 200. Access to treatment, however, is still not available to the most marginalized segments such as commercial sex workers.

The hospital data also point to the severe, toxic effects of ARV drugs. Patients who are poor and malnourished cannot maintain long-term drug adherence. It points to gross and widespread malpractice within the private sector, which is giving patients wrong prescriptions through sub-therapeutic drug combinations and dosages. Data already shows that there is resistance to the first line of ARV drugs and a second line of treatment is now required.

Undoubtedly, patients who seek ARV treatment must have the right to access available treatment especially when it is a matter of life and death. All the same, these drugs do not offer a cure and they are expensive to sustain on a lifelong basis, even when it is the cheaper, generic version. Besides, there is no guarantee of indefinite free supply of antiretroviral therapy and most importantly, it is suicidal to promote it when the infrastructure to administer and monitor it is nonexistent in most developing countries.

For these reasons, ARVs can never be the drug of first choice; the quest for solutions through research in traditional medicines is a crying need of patients in developing countries.

The millions spent in the name of AIDS have facilitated the survival of the AIDS lobby but not the patients.

Sexual Transmission Is Not the Only Factor

There has been far too little analysis of what these strands of information from the ground mean within the wider picture of health. Surely, they force one key question: Assuming that the better off segment of the population is as sexually active (maybe even as promiscuous) as the poor, why are we seeing two different trends, where only the poor are more vulnerable to AIDS?

Is it time to re-evaluate the theory of sexual transmission of this virus as the only factor leading to immune suppression and a disease called AIDS? When we do not have a cure for AIDS, why are we assuming to zero in on only one factor of causation? This rigidity of approach has done great disservice to the cause of public health, including AIDS.

There is a crucial link emerging between nutrition and immunity. A joint statement by two UN agencies—the World Health Organization and the Food and Agriculture Organization—confirms that "A good diet is one of the simplest means of helping people live with HIV/AIDS and may even help delay the progression of the deadly virus . . . The nutritional aspect of HIV/AIDS has been ignored for a long time. The attention was always focused on drugs . . . The message was always: 'Take two tablets after meals.' But they forgot about the meals."

Unfortunately, this insight has not translated into action. For AIDS patients in Mumbai who desperately need access to a nutritious diet of fresh seasonal fruits and green vegetables, such food is a rare luxury. The millions spent in the name of AIDS have facilitated the survival of the AIDS lobby but not the patients. Our policy planning has yet to understand the vital role of local food self-sufficiency, national food sovereignty and public education on what the body needs to stay healthy.

Hopeful Progress Is Being Made Toward an AIDS Vaccine

Khopotso Bodibe

Khopotso Bodibe is a South African radio journalist who has won awards for his reporting on AIDS. In the following viewpoint, he reports that an AIDS vaccine tested in Thailand gave recipients some immunity to the disease. The immunity was not sufficient, but it did suggest direction for future tests, Bodibe says. He notes that scientists have been trying to create an AIDS vaccine for ten years without success. HIV changes and adapts so quickly, scientists note, that a vaccine may need to be altered and administered every year, as with the influenza vaccine.

As you read, consider the following questions:

1. What was the protective rate of the Thai vaccine, according to Bodibe?

2. According to the author's report, why is it important to test the vaccine in South Africa rather than just in Thailand?

3. Lynn Morris says that using two vaccines is helpful because it stimulates what?

Khopotso Bodibe, "Bolstering the Search for HIV Vaccine—Living with AIDS #443," Health-e News Service, August 12, 2010. Copyright © 2010 by Health-e News Service. Reproduced by permission.

Intensifying their search for a vaccine to prevent HIV infection, scientists are planning to run an improved version of the successful Thai HIV vaccine trial in South Africa next year.

News from Thailand late last year that a vaccine trial conducted among 16,000 Thais gave a 31% protection rate against HIV infection has given scientists hope that their quest to find a vaccine to prevent HIV infection is on the horizon. But further tests are needed and South Africa is an obvious place for these to be run, given our high HIV rate.

"There was a clinical trial that was done in Thailand and the results were reported in October last year that, for the first time, showed a hint that we'll be able to protect people from HIV by vaccination. We're really building on those findings and there are big plans to repeat those trials, both in South Africa and elsewhere, and, of course, improve on those, but to really see whether these first signs are really something that we can use to make a better vaccine", explained Lynn Morris, a Wits University professor and researcher for the National Institute for Communicable Diseases (NICD), adding that "the Thai trial showed that the vaccine in question had a protective rate of 31%".

"[A 31% protective rate is] a very low percentage and certainly not high enough for one to implement that vaccine. It's not good enough for use, but it's good enough to explore further."

But "that's a very low percentage and certainly not high enough for one to implement that vaccine. It's not good enough for use, but it's good enough to explore further", Morris said explaining why further studies using the Thai vaccine model will be carried out in South Africa.

"Basically, the way these trials work is that half the people get a placebo or a sugar-coated pill and the other half get the vaccine. In this case it was a huge trial. It was about 16,000 people, so roughly 8,000 in each arm. There were fewer infections in the people who got the vaccine. That's how they calculated the 31%. And there were some indications from the vaccine trial that the protection was more effective early on. So, maybe these vaccines need boosting. That's something that's going to be explored, that, maybe we need to give more immunizations. We certainly need to improve on the vaccines themselves as well. But a very important thing, actually, is that it needs to be tested in different populations. The Thai population was, generally, fairly low-risk, so one of the important things is to test whether this vaccine will work in a high-risk population, and that's why the plan is to do it here in South Africa", she added.

Morris said the Thai study opened up a new path for the future of HIV vaccines development. For the first time scientists studied two vaccines, ALVAC and AIDSVAX, in one trial.

"In fact, it's two different vaccines that were tested. These two vaccines were designed to stimulate two different arms of the immune response. It's what is called a prime-boost approach. You basically prime the immune system with a particular vaccine—and, in this case it was a canary pox-based vaccine—and then you boost that response with a recombinant protein.

For more than a decade scientists have been unable to come up with a successful vaccine against HIV infection.

"I know that probably sounds very technical. . . .What I want to say is the vectored vaccines, basically, are used as vehicles to get small pieces of HIV into the human body and to be taken up by the immune system and to stimulate the cells that fight infection in your body. Now that vaccine has, in fact, been tested previously and shown not to be very effective. And, then, the boost vaccine, which is a protein, has, in fact, also been tested previously and also shown not to be very effective. That vaccine is to stimulate the antibody response in your body. What is interesting about this is that we've basically taken two vaccines that did not show to be very promising on their own and we've combined them. The trick is we are stimulating both arms of the immune response. Previously, the vaccine trials tested only stimulating the antibody response or only stimulating the cellular immune response. We really do need to stimulate multiple arms of the immune response", she said.

For more than a decade scientists have been unable to come up with a successful vaccine against HIV infection. Four efficacy trials have since been conducted worldwide, with the first results being released in 2003. Scientists describe their challenge as "a moving target". They say HIV is able to hide and change its identity, thus making it difficult to attack it. When asked if that does not mean that any attempts at finding an effective vaccine against HIV are not already doomed, Morris replied:

"I think it's important to bear in mind that no vaccine is 100% protective, and particularly, for HIV what that means is behavior change needs to be a permanent change. People have to reduce their risk in order to avoid HIV infection. But in terms of the vaccine, whether we're going to need to make a new vaccine to cope with this changing virus remains to be seen. Influenza is another virus that mutates a lot, and as you know with influenza, we need to make a new vaccine every year so that the vaccine matches the virus that we're going to be exposed to. If you take that paradigm and switch it to HIV, HIV is a far more variable virus than influenza. It's possible that, yes, we're going to have to make a new vaccine on a regular basis in order to deal with that variability".

The Thai vaccine is one of four that will be tested next year. Two others developed in South Africa will also be tested, but only to determine their safety and to see what immune responses they generate in the body. If they are shown to stimulate the right immune responses, they may well also be tested in large-scale efficacy trials in the future.

Drugs Rather than Vaccines May Be the Key to Controlling AIDS

The Economist

The Economist *is a weekly British business and news magazine. In the following viewpoint, it reports that creating an AIDS vaccine is proving difficult. A better approach, it says, might be to make sure to deliver antiretroviral drugs to all of those already infected by the disease. This would make those treated less infectious. According to this model, the* Economist *says, even asymptomatic HIV sufferers would have to be placed on drug regimes. This may be a good idea anyway, it concludes, since some evidence suggests that treatment before symptoms appear greatly improves survival chances.*

As you read, consider the following questions:

1. In a contagious disease, each act of infection involves what two parties, according to the *Economist*?
2. According to Reuben Granich, in an ideal world, who would come in for AIDS testing and how often?
3. Would Dr. Granich's scheme be more or less costly than current AIDS programs in the short and long term?

It has become a cliché among doctors who deal with AIDS that the only way to stop the epidemic is to develop a vaccine against HIV, the virus that causes it. Unfortunately, there is no sign of such a thing becoming available soon. The best hope was withdrawn from trials just over a year ago amid fears that it might actually be making things worse. As a result, vaccine researchers have mostly gone back to the drawing board of basic research. Meanwhile, the virus marches on. Last year [2007], according to UNAIDS, the international body charged with combating it, 2.7m [million] people were infected, bringing the estimated total to 33m.

Treat the Infected

Reuben Granich and his colleagues at the World Health Organization (WHO), though, have been exploring an alternative approach. Instead of a vaccine, they wonder, as they write in the *Lancet*, whether the job might be done with drugs.

In the spread of any contagious disease, each act of infection has two parties, one who already has the disease and one who does not. Vaccination works by treating the uninfected individual prophylactically. Since it is impossible to say in advance who might be exposed, that means vaccinating everybody. The alternative, as Dr Granich observes, is to treat the infected individual and thus stop him being infectious. For this to curb an epidemic would require an enormous public health campaign of the sort used to promote vaccination. But that campaign would be of a different kind. It would have to identify all (or, at least, almost all) of those infected. It would then have to persuade them to undergo not a short, simple vaccination course, but rather a drug regime that would continue indefinitely.

The first question to ask of such an approach is, could it work in principle? It is this [question] that Dr Granich and his colleagues have tried to answer. Using data from several African countries, they have constructed a computer model to test the idea. In their ideal world everyone over the age of 15 would volunteer for testing once a year. If found to be infected, they would be put immediately onto a course of what are known as first-line antiretroviral drugs (ARVs). These are reasonably cheap, often generic, pharmaceuticals that, although they do not cure someone, do lower the level of the virus in his body to the extent that he suffers no symptoms. They also—and this is the point of the study—reduce the level enough to make him unlikely to pass the virus on. For the 3% or so of people per year for whom the first-line ARVs do not work, more expensive second-line treatments would be used.

Within 50 years the prevalence of HIV would drop below 1%, compared with up to 30% at the moment in the worst-affected areas.

When Dr Granich crunched the numbers through the model, he concluded that if this scheme could be implemented, it would do the trick. The rate of new infections (now 20 per 1,000 people per year) would fall within ten years of full implementation to one per 1,000 per year. Within 50 years the prevalence of HIV would drop below 1%, compared with up to 30% at the moment in the worst-affected areas.

Drugs for the Asymptomatic

Whether such an approach could be made to work in practice—and if it could, whether it should—are two other questions. The existing plan for combating HIV centres on saving the lives of those already infected. The intention is to make ARVs available to everyone who needs them, in rich and poor countries alike, by buying the drugs cheaply and building the infrastructure of doctors, nurses and clinics to prescribe and provide them. "Needs", however, is defined as "at risk of developing symptoms". People with HIV often remain asymptomatic for years, and conventional wisdom is that treating such

Estimated Number of AIDS-Related Deaths, in Relation to Prevention Strategy, 2008–2050

Strategy	Deaths	Deaths Averted
No new health strategy	11,078,000	—
Make antiretroviral drugs available to those at earlier stages of HIV	8,658,000	2,419,000
Make antiretroviral drugs available earlier, and institute universal voluntary HIV testing, with antiretroviral therapy for those who test positive	3,879,000	7,199,000

TAKEN FROM: Reuben Granich, "HIV Treatment as Prevention: How Many Lives Could be Saved?" *The Body*, July 20, 2009. www.thebody .com.

people brings little clinical benefit while exposing them to unpleasant side effects such as nausea, vomiting and diarrhoea.

A recent study suggested that deferring treatment until classical symptoms appear increases the chance of someone dying by 70%.

Even vaccination bothers some medical ethicists because, although it does protect the vaccinated individual, governments promote it in order to create "herd immunity"—from which the unvaccinated will also benefit. Treating asymptomatic carriers of HIV causes greater qualms if it brings no benefit to the people actually taking the medicine. However, Kevin De Cock, one of Dr Granich's colleagues, points out that the latest research suggests such people are not as asymptomatic as had once been thought. They may suffer from illnesses such as heart, kidney and liver diseases and cancers that are not classical symptoms of AIDS. Indeed, a recent study suggested that deferring treatment until classical symptoms appear increases the chance of someone dying by 70%.

If that result is confirmed, it would change the ethics completely. It would also make it easier to persuade people to come in once a year for testing at their local clinic, even if they felt well. And it would create pressure for the current policy to be reviewed anyway, so that something like the scheme Dr Granich and his colleagues have been investigating might end up happening by default.

If the scheme were implemented (and the WHO is at pains to point out that this paper in no way indicates a change of policy), it would be more costly to begin with than the existing plan of universal access. However, that would change over the years, as the caseload fell. This seems, therefore, to be an approach worth exploring. AIDS doctors are not so spoilt for options that they can afford to ignore new ones. Employing the logic of vaccination using proven drugs may be an idea whose time has come.

HIV/AIDS Treatment Is Hampered by Lack of Political Will

Kate Kelland

Kate Kelland is a journalist who covers health and science issues. In the following viewpoint, she reports that scientists have developed many effective means of fighting HIV/AIDS. She says these include effective drugs, prevention methods, and other programs. Policy makers, however, have been unwilling to provide the funds necessary to implement these treatments, she writes. As a result, AIDS continues to spread. Scientists are concerned that without more political support and more money, millions will die unnecessarily of AIDS, she reports.

As you read, consider the following questions:

1. According to Michel Sidibe, how many new HIV infections are there in the world per day?

2. What region has the fastest-growing HIV epidemic in the world, according to Kelland?

3. According to the writer, how much did donor governments allocate for AIDS relief in developing nations in 2008 and 2009?

An international AIDS conference has exposed a gulf between scientists and politicians on how to tackle the deadly HIV pandemic.

More Funding Is Needed

Despite promises from governments around the world to pursue evidence-based policies, AIDS experts are frustrated at a refusal to adapt to new ways of looking at HIV and the people most at risk of contracting it.

It is a stance that displays discrimination and criminal negligence, says Julio Montaner, president of the International AIDS Society, who has led a drive at the conference to get politicians to wake up to the evidence.

"Yes we are treating five million people today, but there are 10 million people who need treatment, otherwise they will get sick and die. Not treating them amounts to criminal negligence," he told Reuters.

The message from scientists is: We've given you the tools and the evidence, now give us the money to use them.

At the heart of scientists' frustration is the impressive progress made against the human immunodeficiency virus (HIV) that causes AIDS since it emerged in the early 1980s.

Advances in medicines have effectively turned an acute killer disease into a manageable chronic condition in many wealthy countries. Patients who take cocktails of AIDS drugs can often live normal lives—they work, have sex, bear children and can even look forward to meeting their grandchildren.

The message from scientists is: We've given you the tools and the evidence, now give us the money to use them.

Yet the political will to fund the AIDS battle is waning, they say.

"The world has become numb to the toll of 7,400 new HIV infections every day," said Michel Sidibe, director of the

Joint United Nations Programme on AIDS (UNAIDS). "We need to recover our sense of outrage."

The AIDS virus infects 33.4 million people globally. In sub-Saharan Africa, 22.4 million people have it. Eastern Europe has the fastest-growing HIV epidemic in the world.

So while the disease has been contained in some groups, in others the epidemic is raging "out of control," according to one World Health Organization expert. Other analysts at the conference described the situation as "like running after an accelerating train."

The Epidemic Is Growing

"Today, for every two persons starting treatment, five new infections occur," Françoise Barré-Sinoussi, the French scientist who won a Nobel prize in 2008 for her work in identifying HIV in 1983, told the Vienna conference.

"The growing curve of the epidemic cannot be stopped without a strong and global commitment to combined HIV prevention measures, including treatment."

The Vienna conference has seen study after study on HIV prevention measures ranging from male circumcision to microbicide gels containing AIDS drugs.

Studies on Eastern Europe have found harsh laws and authorities' refusal to offer HIV services to injecting drug users are fuelling an underground epidemic there.

Overall support for the AIDS fight from donor nations flattened last year [2009] amid the financial crisis.

In Africa, researchers have demonstrated treatment programmes which cut costs by simplifying the ways in which patients get their drugs and earlier treatment.

UNAIDS has drawn up proposals called "Treatment 2.0" designed to improve efficiency in the global AIDS effort by developing more simplified drugs and delivery systems and using more community health workers.

But UNAIDS also reported that overall support for the AIDS fight from donor nations flattened last year [2009] amid the financial crisis.

In 2009, the G8 [a group of eight countries] leading wealthy nations, the European Commission and other donor governments provided $7.6 billion for AIDS relief in developing nations, compared with $7.7 billion disbursed in 2008.

The head of the Global Fund to Fight AIDS, Tuberculosis and Malaria, Michel Kazatchkine, says he is "really afraid" about the prospect of getting the $20 billion needed to continue the AIDS battle for the next three years.

"The big frustration is that we feel we have really responded to the call of proving certain efficiency models," said Nathan Ford, a Médecins Sans Frontières doctor who works on AIDS treatment programmes in some of Africa's poorest countries.

"I get the sense that no amount of data is going to change things. The decision has already been taken—but that is not how global health should be run."

A replenishment conference is due on October 5 [2010] in New York. Until then, Kazatchkine says there is time to show political leaders how the evidence is stacking up to show not increasing AIDS funding will be a decision that costs millions of lives.

"We have demonstrated the feasibility. Countries have shown that they can massively scale up. The case is strong. The funding decision is a political decision for the leaders of this world, and a political decision is a choice," he said.

Brazil Needs to Alter Its Policy on Providing Anti-AIDS Drugs

Alexandre Grangeiro, Luciana Teixeira, Francisco I. Bastos, and Paulo Teixeira

Alexandre Grangeiro and Paulo Teixeira are members of the office of the Secretary of Health of São Paulo; Luciana Teixeira is a professor of economics at the University of Brazil; Francisco I. Bastos is with the Center of Information, Science, and Technology in Rio de Janeiro. In the following viewpoint, the authors argue that acquiring antiretroviral drugs is becoming more and more expensive in Brazil. As a result, they conclude, Brazil's policy of providing universal access to antiretroviral drugs is unsustainable.

As you read, consider the following questions:

1. According to the authors, how much have STD/AIDS programs saved Brazil between 1997 and 2003?
2. Are antiretroviral drug prices in Brazil lower or higher than those observed worldwide, according to the authors?
3. At what rate do the authors say Brazil would have to grow over the next three years if the drug policy is to be sustainable?

Alexandre Grangeiro, Luciana Teixeira, Francisco I. Bastos, and Paulo Teixeira, "Sustainability of Brazilian Policy for Access to Antiretroviral Drugs," *Revista de Saúde Pública*, vol. 40, supp., April 2006, pp. 2–3, 7–9. Copyright © *Revista de Saúde Pública* 2006. Reproduced by permission.

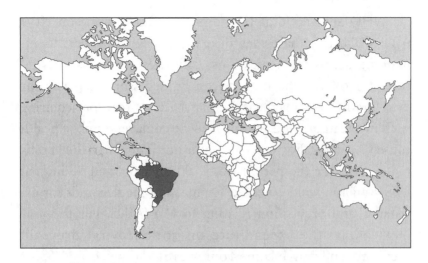

The Declaration of Commitment on HIV/AIDS adopted at the Special Session of the United Nations that was held in New York in July 2001 established as one of its principles that people living with HIV and AIDS should have access to anti-retroviral drugs. In the chapter "Care, Support and Treatment", countries took on the commitment to create national strategies by the year 2003, to deal with and if possible overcome the various obstacles that affect the supply of these drugs. For 2005, countries were called on to make investments aimed at expanding care and access to drugs.

Improvement in Health

The adoption of these targets at a global level is important for reducing the impact of the epidemic, particularly in countries that present structural deficiencies and large-magnitude epidemics. According to the World Health Organization (WHO), 3 million people die as a result of AIDS every year. Around 80% of them did not have the benefit of the drug therapies available. Although advances have taken place over the last few years, the situation in December 2005 in poor and developing countries was that, out of the 6.5 million individuals who required such treatment, only 1.3 million were receiving it.

WHO and the Joint United Nations Programme on HIV/ AIDS (UNAIDS) have identified the following barriers to expanding access to medications: countries' inadequate structures for offering health services; limited world capacity for drug production; insufficient financial resources for acquiring such medications; and the consequent damage to public health caused by inequality and social injustice. There have been estimates that, for the period from 2005 to 2008, an additional US$18 billion will be needed for meeting the demands for assistance and prevention relating to HIV/AIDS. For the year 2008 alone, the expenditure on antiretroviral drugs in medium- and low-income countries is estimated as US$5.2 billion.

The Brazilian policy for access to antiretroviral drugs started to be implemented in 1991, offering the drug zidovudine (AZT). Today, 16 drugs are available within the health system. Decisions on incorporating new antiretrovirals within the Brazilian national health system [Sistema Único de Saúde] (SUS) are made following technical analysis carried out by three advisory committees, which are also responsible for the recommendations for the use and monitoring of these medications.

From an economic point of view, it is undeniable that access to antiretrovirals has caused a reduction in the expenditure on hospitalization and therapeutic procedures.

Just as in developed countries and in the few other developing countries that have expanded access to antiretrovirals, the policy for universal access to medications in Brazil has generated unequivocal benefits. These have occurred both within the collective sphere (through reducing the infectiousness of people living with HIV/AIDS, this contributes towards controlling the epidemic), and at the individual level (through causing substantial increases in the survival and quality of life of people with HIV and AIDS).

Other benefits that are still partial have been observed in relation to improvement of the structure and operation of the Brazilian health system. The AIDS program has functioned as a paradigm for how the Brazilian health system should operate with regard to awareness-raising campaigns, partnership with civil society, supply of materials and careful monitoring. From an economic point of view, it is undeniable that access to antiretrovirals has caused a reduction in the expenditure on hospitalization and therapeutic procedures. An estimate from the National STD/AIDS Program has indicated savings of more than US$2 billion over the period from 1997 to 2003.

Trying to Ensure Access to Drugs

Despite these results, people living with HIV and AIDS and non-governmental organizations (NGO) have warned that the sustainability of the policy of universal access is at risk, as a result of the progressive increase in expenditure on the acquisition of antiretrovirals. In 2005, the National Health Council recommended that the Ministry of Health should adopt a system of compulsory licensing of imported medications, in order to reduce the spending resulting from this policy.

The reasons for the increase in this spending are: the growth in the number of people with HIV/AIDS undergoing treatment; the emergence of viral resistance, which means that patients have to be treated using more expensive medications, the so-called second-line drugs; the incorporation of new drugs with higher prices than those that are already available in the therapeutic arsenal; the Industrial Property Law, which restricts the production of generic versions of original medications that came onto the market after 1996; and the limited capacity of national industry to produce new generic medications in the event of the approval of a compulsory license.

Brazil's Success Against AIDS

The first case of AIDS was recorded in Brazil in 1982, and whilst many countries have struggled to curb the spread of HIV and to care for those with AIDS, Brazil's response has been seen as a success story. Working alongside civil society groups, the Brazilian government has made aggressive efforts to minimise the impact of the AIDS epidemic. By the end of 2007, 730,000 Brazilians were living with HIV—just over half the number that estimates in the previous decade had predicted. The AIDS mortality rate has fallen and the number of people who avoided hospital due to effective treatment saved over US$2 billion in medical costs between 1996 and 2004. HIV prevalence has remained at 0.6 percent since 2004.

Avert, "HIV & AIDS in Brazil." www.avert.org.

The discussion on the sustainability of the Brazilian policy involves international questions, especially since the main raw material-producing countries adopted national legislation on intellectual property rights in the field of pharmaceuticals, in consonance with accords established within the context of the World Trade Organization. The expectation is that the adoption of these laws—especially by India, in 2005, and almost simultaneously by China—will limit the worldwide production of generics and produce an impact on the drug market, thus making it difficult to obtain reductions in the prices of these products in poor and developing countries.

In this respect, the organization Médecins Sans Frontières has warned about the "crisis of second-line drugs". According to this NGO, incorporation of therapeutic schemes using more expensive medications will have a financial impact on the access programs. Consequently, developing countries will have great difficulty in ensuring treatment for patients using these new products.

To respond to the problem of sustainability, the Brazilian government has adopted a variety of strategies, among [them]: production of generic medications; price negotiations with pharmaceutical companies; alteration of the national legislation relating to compulsory licensing; and international action aimed at establishing a consensus that would define access to medications as a question of human rights. The solutions that may be adopted in Brazil will have relevance internationally and will serve as a reference for other developing countries. . . .

---

*Consequently, developing countries will have great diffi-
culty in ensuring treatment for patients using these new
products.*

Expenditures Are Rising

The Ministry of Health's increased spending on acquiring AIDS medications in the year 2005 interrupted a historical series characterized by a trend towards stabilization of such expenditure, despite the increase in the numbers of patients undergoing treatment and the inclusion of new drugs . . . during this period. In 2005, the percentages of GDP [gross domestic product] and federal health expenditure committed to purchasing antiretrovirals reached a peak, returning to the levels seen at the end of the 1990s. . . .

In summary, the present study has shown that the incorporation of new drugs that are protected by patents and the increase in the numbers of patients using antiretrovirals are insufficient to explain the increase in expenditure over the period analyzed. The changes in spending observed were associated with effective and efficient adoption of a set of strategies for reducing drug prices. In this respect, the following can be cited: negotiations with pharmaceutical companies; the existence of national industry capable of developing generic drugs; and the government decision to utilize prerogatives within the Intellectual Property Law when necessary. The sustainability of the policy for universal access will therefore depend on the efficiency and effectiveness of government action in using these strategies.

The increase in the prices of generic AIDS medications in Brazil has gone against the international trend.

The study has also shown evidence of weakening of the national generic drug-producing industry over the last few years. As a result of this, there have been increases in the prices of nationally produced medications, failures in the supply of generic and similar drugs in the years 2004 and 2005, and reductions in the scientific and technological capacity of these companies, demonstrated by the lack of incorporation of new generic drugs after the year 2001.

The increase in the prices of generic AIDS medications in Brazil has gone against the international trend. Data from the World Health Organization, corroborated by studies by the organization Médecins Sans Frontières, have shown that, between 2003 and 2005, the prices of first-line medications, composed fundamentally of drugs with generic versions, were reduced by between 37% and 53%, depending on the treatment combination adopted.

The increase in the prices of nationally produced medications has made the prices maintained in Brazil higher than those in the international market today, different to what was observed in the year 2000, according to data from the Ministry of Health and surveys carried out by Médecins Sans Frontières. In 2000, only one of the six generic or similar drugs for adults utilized in Brazil had a higher price than those in other countries, but in 2005, nine out of the eleven drugs offered for treatments had prices higher than those maintained on the international market. Whereas in 2000 the mean price of medications produced in Brazil corresponded to 91.8% of the price for generic drugs commercialized internationally, in 2005 the Brazilian prices were on average three times higher than the lowest prices observed worldwide.

The Policy Cannot Be Sustained

Furthermore, it is emphasized that the results from price negotiations depend on the real capacity for national production of patented drugs, insofar as this allows the differential in prices between patented medications and those produced in this country to be made clear. It has to be stressed that national production is not totally limited by the intellectual property law. The development and registration of generic drugs, according to Brazilian legislation and the World Trade Organization, can take place while a patent is in force, but their commercial limitation is limited.

Alternatively, the strengthening of the national industry could take place through the development of drugs that are not protected by patents, as has been the case with enteric didanosine (DDI), or by means of combinations of generic drugs. Approximately 80% of all medications commercialized around the world are not subject to patents and could be produced nationally.

The sustainability of the policy for access to antiretroviral drugs will only be ensured if the country grows at an annual rate of 6% over the next three years, a scenario that has been shown to be unlikely.

Non-utilization of the prerogatives provided for in the accords on intellectual property, such as compulsory licensing, may also have contributed towards increasing the expenditure on antiretrovirals. The government altered the legislation on this matter in 2003, to allow the importation of generic medications, and in 2004 decreed that lopinavir/ritonavir was a medication of "public utility", which is the first legal stage towards compulsory licensing. The lack of greater political determination within the government, in this respect, weakened the Ministry of Health's negotiating power, and also cast doubt on the capacity to produce new drugs nationally.

The trend towards setting aside increased proportions of GDP and federal health expenditure for acquiring antiretrovirals demonstrates that the sustainability of the policy for access to antiretroviral drugs will only be ensured if the country grows at an annual rate of 6% over the next three years, a scenario that has been shown to be unlikely. Alternatively, it could be ensured if portions of the budget destined for other health actions and AIDS control actions were redirected, and/or if there were the political will to promote the strengthening of the national generics industry, with the aim of achieving reductions in drug prices.

Periodical and Internet Sources Bibliography

The following articles have been selected to supplement the diverse views presented in this chapter.

BBC News	"Brazil to Break AIDS Drugs Patents," December 1, 2004.
Daily Nation	"Deal Spells Doom for Our Chronically Sick," December 12, 2010.
John Donnelly	"AIDS Drugs Hit Roadblock in Africa," *Boston Globe*, June 20, 2005.
Celia W. Dugger	"African Studies Give Women Hope in HIV Fight," *New York Times*, July 19, 2010.
Economist	"AIDS Vaccines: A Fluttering in the Breeze," September 3, 2009.
Marco Evers	"The Quack in Gambia: African Despot 'Cures' AIDS," *Spiegel*, March 8, 2007.
Donald G. McNeil Jr.	"In Uganda, AIDS War Is Falling Apart," *New York Times*, May 9, 2010.
John Moore and Nicoli Nattrass	"Deadly Quackery," *New York Times*, June 4, 2006.
National Institute of Allergy and Infectious Diseases	"NIAID HIV Vaccine Research: A Year in Review, Looking Ahead," June 28, 2010. www.niaid.nih.gov.
Christian Nordqvist	"Global AIDS Deaths and New HIV Cases Dropping, but Funding Shortage Alarming," *Medical News Today*, November 23, 2010.
Spiegel	"AIDS Expert on HIV Prevention Pill: 'Forgoing Condoms Would Be Fatal,'" December 1, 2010.

GLOBALVIEWPOINTS

CHAPTER 3

Moral Issues and HIV/AIDS

Prosecuting Canadians Who Fail to Disclose HIV/AIDS Is Moral

Rosie DiManno

Rosie DiManno is a columnist for the Star *(Toronto). In the following viewpoint, she discusses Johnson Aziga, a Canadian man with HIV who failed to inform sexual partners of his condition and infected many of them. DiManno argues that Aziga's actions were immoral and cruel and resulted in the deaths of at least two women and the infection of others. DiManno concludes that Aziga's conviction for murder and assault was just.*

As you read, consider the following questions:

1. According to DiManno, what were the specific counts on which Aziga was convicted?

2. According to the Crown prosecutors, even if the women he slept with tested negative for HIV, Aziga was guilty of aggravated sexual assault for what reason?

3. Why do some AIDS activists support the view that HIV-positive individuals have no obligation to reveal their status to sexual partners?

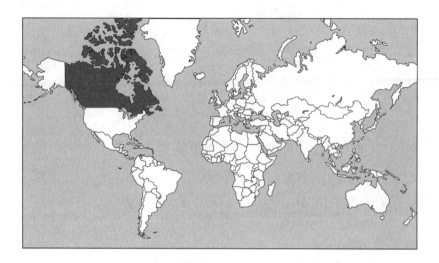

When he wasn't busy fornicating them *to death*, Johnson Aziga must have hated women.

Reckless Transmission

Alternatively, the former Ontario civil servant was entirely indifferent to females, without feeling or conscience as he introduced a silent killer—cloaked in lust—into their lives.

Dishonest and duplicitous, thinking only of his immediate sexual gratification, the 52-year-old knowingly and intentionally exposed his unsuspecting lovers to the HIV virus right up until the morning of his arrest on Aug. 30, 2003.

He cut a wide swath with his penis.

Thinking only of his immediate sexual gratification, the 52-year-old knowingly and intentionally exposed his unsuspecting lovers to the HIV virus.

On Saturday [April 4, 2009], after deliberating for three days, a Hamilton jury found Aziga guilty on two counts of first-degree murder, 10 counts of aggravated sexual assault and one count of attempted aggravated sexual assault.

It was a historic verdict: The first time in Canada—or anywhere in the world, as far as the prosecution is aware—that a criminal case involving the reckless transmission of HIV has resulted in a murder conviction.

Deliberate, without prophylactic protection, done in full awareness that infection of others might result, withholding his HIV-positive status and repeatedly denying his condition to sexual partners who inquired.

Two of those women subsequently died from AIDS-related lymphoma, their videotaped testimony—given shortly before they passed away—played for the jury.

Five other women have tested positive for HIV, the virus that causes AIDS. Four more women have tested negative. But it's still aggravated sexual assault because, as the Crown successfully argued, valid consent cannot be given when information about a partner's diagnosed HIV-positive status has been withheld.

There is an obligation, legally and morally, to disclose.

Aziga did not tell and, further, denied it when directly quizzed by girlfriends who were persuaded to cease using condoms.

All the while, Aziga was receiving antiretroviral therapy to control the advance of his illness. Early detection is crucial for treatment of HIV, modern drugs now extremely effective as intervention, such that the virus is no longer a looming death sentence.

Aziga never gave his many lovers that benefit. He, however, appears perfectly healthy, continuing his drug regimen through the nearly six years thus far spent in custody.

Guilty of First-Degree Murder

Now, he will likely die in prison: First-degree murder means a mandatory life sentence, with no parole eligibility for 25 years.

The trial took five years to come to court, Aziga firing several lawyers along the way, and six months to conclude. Aziga never did take the stand in his own defence. But he'd hardly been a mute defendant. Superior Court Justice Thomas Lofchik allowed the separated father of three to indulge in oratory during earlier phases of the judicial proceeding, which could not be reported at the time.

In late 2006, Aziga—who often scoured legal textbooks in court—mounted his own arguments in opposition to the criminalizing of HIV transmission.

"This is an issue in which it takes two to tango, the sex issue," he expounded. "Somebody may be . . . fraudulent and so mean, but it takes two. It's unfortunate, some people are being reported dead . . . As I said, this is a statement of frustration, not necessarily of anger, especially when you see the exercise that is going on. When we are talking about somebody dying, trying to see whether it should be accepted (as evidence) or not."

Shockingly, there are some AIDS activists who support the view that HIV-positive individuals have no obligation to reveal their status to sexual partners.

Shockingly, there are some AIDS activists who support the view that HIV-positive individuals have no obligation to reveal their status to sexual partners; that everyone is responsible for taking their own precautions. One school of thought contends that criminalizing even reckless behaviour will discourage people from being tested for HIV as a pre-emptive legal defence: They didn't know they were infected, so can't be held accountable for passing on the virus.

Aziga was diagnosed with HIV in 1996. He received counselling from medical staff on both safe-sex practices and his legal obligation to disclose positive status to sexual partners. Fully educated about the virus, Aziga nevertheless continued his reckless behaviour before and after separating from his wife. Twice he was issued with orders under the Health Pro-

tection and Promotion Act to abstain from sex involving pe-
nile penetration unless he disclosed his HIV and wore a latex
condom "from onset of erection."

Following his arrest—his photo circulated in the media—
several other women came forward to lodge complaints with
police. In the end, there were 13 complainants, though two
were dropped en route to trial.

The Crown presented evidence that all the women contracted an HIV strain from a shared source, a strain rare in
North America but common in areas of Africa. Aziga hails
from Uganda.

He liked his women white, plain, even homely and probably lonely. They were co-workers, single-mom neighbours
and ladies picked up in bars.

Of course, to make love is not necessarily to like and clearly
not to give a damn.

Prosecuting Germans Who Fail to Disclose HIV/AIDS Is Not Moral

Gisela Friedrichsen

Gisela Friedrichsen is a German journalist. In the following viewpoint, she reports that as a teen, German pop star Nadja Benaissa failed to inform sexual partners that she was HIV positive. Friedrichsen argues that prosecutors who charged Benaissa acted irresponsibly and sensationally. Friedrichsen notes that Benaissa has expressed regret about her actions and that there is evidence that she now routinely informs sexual partners about her infection. Given her youth at the time of the incident and her expressions of regret, Friedrichsen concludes, Benaissa should be treated leniently by the court.

As you read, consider the following questions:

1. According to the author, where was Benaissa arrested?
2. What did doctors tell Benaissa about the risks of infecting others, according to the singer?
3. What sentence does Friedrichsen think Benaissa will receive?

The trial of German pop star Nadja Benaissa, who is accused of infecting a sexual partner with HIV, is the culmination of a witch hunt against the singer. The case revolves

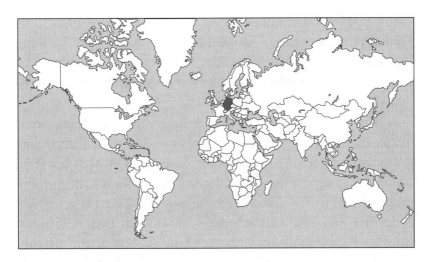

around the question of who is responsible for safe sex and whether Benaissa, who was only 16 when she learned her HIV status, was a victim of the pressure of the music industry.

The Prosecution Is a Witch Hunt

Perhaps the case could have been settled with a simple penalty order, which would have avoided a trial. But that would only have been possible if five men—a circuit judge, a chief prosecutor, an official solicitor and two detective superintendents—had not met on April 2 of last year [2009] at the district attorney's office in the western German city of Darmstadt and decided to give the case such a high profile. Or if they had later found their way back to a more levelheaded approach. But once it had been set in motion, the stigmatizing witch hunt had to run its course.

During that fateful meeting in Darmstadt, the five men agreed on how they would proceed in the case of the German pop singer Nadja Benaissa, who is a member of the band No Angels, Germany's biggest girl group. In June 2008, a former boyfriend had accused Benaissa, who is HIV-positive, of infecting him with the virus by having unprotected sex with him four years earlier. On the evening of April 12 of last year, the defendant was to be arrested during a performance at the Frankfurt music venue "Nachtleben" and immediately brought before an investigating judge. For someone who had hoped to provoke a spectacular case, the charges against the celebrity pop star came at an opportune time.

On April 9, 2009, the chief prosecutor and the circuit judge discussed the planned arrest once again. Realizing that the singer's place of residence was "unclear" and that her performance in Frankfurt would be the only opportunity to apprehend her, they made a slight change to their plan. Instead of having Benaissa arrested after the concert, they decided it would be preferable to make their move before the performance. Fearing an angry reaction from her loyal fans, they also decided to avoid having her taken away through the crowd.

Once it had been set in motion, the stigmatizing witch hunt had to run its course.

Instead, Benaissa was arrested near the entrance to the club, where fans were waiting in line for tickets—a move clearly intended to stir up publicity. The investigating judge immediately ordered that Benaissa be remanded in custody. Apparently no one felt it was necessary to consider whether it was appropriate to take Benaissa into custody on the strength of a suspicion that allegedly stemmed from an incident that had happened five years earlier.

The Darmstadt district attorney's office launched its second offensive on the first business day after Easter. Although it didn't provide the name of the singer in a press release it issued that day (her identity was already widely known after the Frankfurt arrest), it did state she was HIV-positive and that she was suspected of having "had unprotected sexual intercourse with three individuals in 2004 and 2006," and that she had allegedly failed to inform her partners about her infection. "With at least one of the partners, a test showed that he—presumably as a result of the contact—is now also HIV-positive," said district attorney Ger Neuber.

The investigators claim that the police had tried to approach the singer for months. "After that, we initiated further investigations when it became known, in the late phase of the undertaking, that two other men had also allegedly had unprotected sex with her," said Neuber. "This meant that there was a strong suspicion that she had committed a crime and that there was a risk of re-offending."

The tabloid newspaper *Bild* asked the logical question: "How many men has No Angels star Nadja infected?" And then it reassured its readers by writing: "Now Nadja is in pretrial detention on suspicion of aggravated battery, to protect other men against infection!"

The disclosure of the most intimate details of the singer's sex life and, most of all, the questionable use of the "risk of re-offending" to justify her arrest—whatever happened to the presumption of innocence?—sparked a heated debate in the ensuing months among members of the legal system, the media and politicians. Suddenly the courts were barring reporting on a case that prosecutors had already deliberately thrust into the limelight. Whether the Benaissa case was truly about aggravated battery and the question of who had infected whom, which was completely unresolved at the time—all of this was drowned out by the dispute over the limits of judicial public relations and the "pressing public need" to know "when someone uses her body as a biological weapon," in the words of Siegmund Ehrmann, a member of the German parliament for the center-left Social Democratic Party.

Benaissa Did Not Intend to Infect Others

Now Benaissa is being tried in a juvenile court in Darmstadt, charged with one count of aggravated battery and three of attempted battery. On the first day of the trial, her lawyer, Oliver Wallasch, who appeared to be treating her gently as he accompanied her to the court, submitted a statement for his client in which he stated that the charges were "probably correct." Wallasch also stated that it was true that the defendant had known that she was HIV-positive since 1999, the year her daughter was born.

But doctors had apparently assured her that the risk of acquiring AIDS was close to zero, provided she remained sufficiently disciplined and remained under constant medical supervision. According to the statement, the doctors had told Benaissa that this also applied to the risk of infection "if the viral load was undetectable."

"I trusted those doctors," Benaissa insisted. But, she added, she "wrongly and, in retrospect, more than negligently" pushed the residual risk to the back of her mind and told herself that she would never become sick.

Benaissa argued that she had never intended to infect someone else with the virus, and that she had always insisted that her partners use condoms.

Then she addressed a sensitive issue. "I also thought that my respective partners also bore some of the responsibility to talk about and contribute to preventing infection by using condoms. In this respect, I neglected my own responsibility. Today I have to admit that this was a big mistake on my part."

Aggravated battery is an intentional crime. This means that the Darmstadt juvenile court and its presiding judge, Dennis Wacker, will have to prove that the defendant knew about the risk of infecting her sex partners and accepted the possibility of infection.

Speaking through her attorney, Benaissa argued that she had never intended to infect someone else with the virus, and that she had always insisted that her partners use condoms. But "in some cases the partners dealt with the issue in a com-

---

Limit Criminalization of HIV Transmission

In some countries, criminal law is being applied to those who transmit or expose others to HIV infection. There are no data indicating that the broad application of criminal law to HIV transmission will achieve either criminal justice or prevent HIV transmission. Rather, such application risks undermining public health and human rights. Because of these concerns, UNAIDS [the Joint United Nations Programme on HIV/AIDS] urges governments to limit criminalization to cases of intentional transmission, i.e. where a person knows his or her HIV positive status, acts with the intention to transmit HIV, and does in fact transmit it.

In other instances, the application of criminal law should be rejected by legislators, prosecutors and judges.

UNAIDS, Criminalization of HIV Transmission: Policy Brief, *August 2008. http://unaids.org.*

---

pletely careless way." The question is: Should she have been equally casual about accepting their behavior?

Men tend to leave contraception up to women, be it prevention of an unwanted pregnancy or avoiding infection. Their sex partners often seek to excuse their behavior with the argument that they were young and were drunk on the evening or night in question, and that "it just happened."

Listening to the Wrong Advisers

In light of what Benaissa says about the music industry and its countless advisers and so-called artist agents, who take advantage of young girls by promising them a big career, she apparently now knows that she listened to too many of the wrong advisers.

She had recently given birth to her child, at the age of 16, and had hardly recovered from her drug addiction and a miserable life on the street when she found out that she was HIV-positive. And before she could even understand what this meant, she was already a star in the limelight, sexy, glitzy and euphoric, surrounded by hysterical fans. "A week later, I didn't know what I wanted anymore," she told the court.

Is she trying to protect herself when she says that she ignored the risks? She was little more than a child when she received the shocking diagnosis. Is it something a 16-year-old girl is even equipped to handle?

She had recently given birth to her child, at the age of 16, and had hardly recovered from her drug addiction and a miserable life on the street when she found out that she was HIV-positive.

Naturally she didn't want anyone to find out about the infection, and naturally she felt ashamed. There was a lot at stake: the band's career and the money it stood to earn. Naturally, she was under pressure from the advisers and agents, who stood to make money with her and the other girls. And of course she was afraid and sought to numb her fears with success, allowed others to control her and dictate her role to her, all in an effort to escape the truth. But should she have kept her silence when she was about to have sex with someone who didn't want to use a condom? Shouldn't she have disclosed her status?

She described how the rumor that "Nadja is positive" was spread on the social networking website Facebook when the band made its comeback, and how others looked askance at her and whispered behind her back. It was revealed during the trial that a newspaper had tried to force her to come clean, and that there had been blackmail threats. "I was being terrorized from all sides," Benaissa said. "It was simply too much for me, having to do everything right in that situation." All of this may be true. But it's also true that, in the public's perception, HIV infection is still equated with AIDS, while the person who is infected can feel perfectly healthy.

Testimony from Former Boyfriends

The man she allegedly infected is six years older than Benaissa. He has known since 2007 that he is infected with the possibly deadly virus. His life has become unhinged as a result.

During the trial, he spoke disparagingly of "her over there," or referred to her sarcastically as "that nice lady" who has "brought so much suffering into the world." His voice was full of loathing and thinly veiled hate. He said things that no man should say about a woman. He tried to maintain his composure. When he was asked when he found that he too was HIV-positive, it doesn't take him long to answer, as if the date and place had been burned into his mind: "Paris, Feb. 7, 2007."

"My impression was that she handled the infection very responsibly," he said.

On Wednesday [August 2010], an expert from the University of Munich will explain to the court whether it is in fact possible to trace the man's infection to the defendant. There have been significant advances in the study of HIV recently. Perhaps it will soon be possible to keep an HIV infection under such control with drugs that the risk of infection is virtually eliminated. But science hadn't reached that stage yet when Benaissa was having unprotected sex.

One of the first witnesses to testify was a 38-year-old musician who was friends with the defendant between 2003 and 2004. She trusted him and told him that she was HIV-positive. "My impression was that she handled the infection very responsibly," he said. He added that they spoke about it openly, and that when the friendship turned into a relationship, there was no question that they used condoms. Another 37-year-old man who had had an on-off relationship with Benaissa between 1999 and 2001 told the court on Monday that Benaissa had informed him about her HIV status on the evening they first met and had always insisted on using condoms. In other words, responsible sex was apparently also an option for Benaissa.

The verdict in the case is expected on Thursday. In recent days, some voices in the media have predicted that Benaissa will probably end up with a 10-year prison sentence. But this seems unlikely, given the way the trial has been going. The prosecution, the defense, the lawyers for the joint plaintiff and the court are clearly making an effort to bring the overinflated case back down to earth.

If she is sentenced to probation, no one need worry that this young woman will ever use her body as a "biological weapon" again.

Iran's Moral Flexibility Has Helped the Fight Against AIDS

Karl Vick

Karl Vick is a journalist who has written for the Washington Post *and* Time. *In the following viewpoint, he reports that AIDS in Iran is rising dangerously among drug users. Despite the fact that Iran is run by religious fundamentalists, Vick says, the government has begun to offer heroin addicts clean needles and methadone. Vick notes that the Iranian attitude is actually more liberal than the drug policies in the United States. He concludes that Iran's flexibility toward drug users should be very helpful in the fight against AIDS.*

As you read, consider the following questions:

1. According to Vick, officials in Iran were alarmed by what rate of HIV infection among hard-core heroin users?

2. How much do drug users pay for a syringe in Iran, according to Azarakhsh Mokri?

3. When and why does Vick say that heroin use increased dramatically in Iran?

Fearing an AIDS epidemic, Iran's theocratic government has dropped a zero-tolerance policy against increasingly common heroin use and now offers addicts low-cost needles, methadone and a measure of social acceptance.

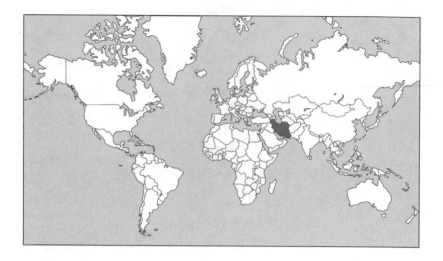

Targeting Drug Users for Help

For two decades, Iran largely avoided the global AIDS crisis. But today, officials are alarmed by a 25 percent HIV infection rate that one survey has found among hard-core heroin users and worry that addicts may channel the virus into the population of 68 million.

Supporters of the government's new approach laud it as practical and devoid of the wishful thinking and moralism that they contend hampers policies on drug abuse and AIDS in some other countries, including the United States. "I have to pay tribute to Iran on this," said Roberto Arbitrio, head of the [United Nations] Office on Drugs and Crime in Tehran.

Bijan Nasirimanesh, who heads a drop-in clinic that dispenses needles, bleach and methadone in a hard-hit area of south Tehran, said, "It's ironic that Iran, very fundamentalist, very religious—very religious—has been able to convince itself" to embrace such policies.

Opponents often argue that tolerance of life-destroying drugs is simply unacceptable and in the long run breeds acceptance and higher drug use. But in the theocracy's most dramatic rejection of that approach, the ayatollah [a Muslim religious title] who heads Iran's conservative judiciary issued an executive order embracing "such needed and fruitful programs" as needle exchanges and methadone maintenance.

Ayatollah Mohammad Esmail Shoshtari, the justice minister who has shut more than 100 newspapers and imprisoned political opponents, instructed prosecutors in a Jan. 24 [2005] letter to ignore laws on the books and defer to Iran's Health Ministry to counter the spread of AIDS and hepatitis C.

"This was a very crucial step," said Ali Hashemi, director of Iran's Drug Control Headquarters, a cabinet-level office. "Inevitably we have to do this in order to reduce the risk of AIDS."

The ayatollah who heads Iran's conservative judiciary issued an executive order embracing "such needed and fruitful programs" as needle exchanges and methadone maintenance.

Surprising Flexibility

The policy demonstrates the complexities of Iran a quarter-century after the Islamic revolution and U.S. Embassy takeover that still defines its theocratic government for many Americans. Though power remains concentrated in unelected clerics who brook little political dissent, the government has demonstrated flexibility on a variety of subjects, including birth control and sex-change operations, which the clerics recently authorized.

After the revolution [in 1979], Iran treated drug users as criminals, throwing hundreds of thousands of them in jail. Now it has joined the ranks of countries that acknowledge the difficulty of eradicating drug addiction and focus instead on curbing the most immediate dangerous behaviors that go with it.

Surveys of Iranians who test positive for HIV show that two-thirds were infected by dirty needles. To reduce the spread of infections, the government not only makes needles available without a prescription, but through subsidies makes them extremely cheap, so as to discourage re-use.

"You pay less than 5 cents for a syringe," said Azarakhsh Mokri, of the government's National Center for Addiction Studies. "People purchase up to 100 at a time."

The government also encourages addicts to stop injecting by providing free methadone, a surrogate opiate that is taken orally. This spring, the parliament, dominated by conservatives, voted to allow any doctor in Iran to dispense methadone, though under strict monitoring guidelines.

To reduce the spread of infections, the government not only makes needles available without a prescription, but through subsidies makes them extremely cheap, so as to discourage re-use.

"It's quite amazing there's been this shift," said Rich Schottenfeld, a professor of psychiatry at Yale University, which won a waiver from U.S. sanctions on Iran to carry out a study financed by the National Institute on Drug Abuse to compare drug treatments. "Five years ago, my colleagues there didn't anticipate that methadone would even be allowed," he said.

Robert Newman, director of the Baron Edmond de Rothschild Chemical Dependency Institute of Beth Israel Medical Center in New York, said Iranian policies are "in very dramatic contrast to what has been happening with increasing frequency in America, where the judiciary and the criminal justice system in general . . . does not let the patients receive the treatment that the physician says is necessary."

Newman, who has traveled twice to Iran in the last five years to consult on addiction programs, said only a quarter of an estimated 900,000 heroin addicts in the United States receive treatment. He attributes that in large part to laws that restrict methadone to large-scale treatment facilities. "In other

Iran's Drug Problem

Iran has an estimated 3 million drug users and "by many accounts, the world's worst heroin problem," says Peter Reuter, . . . professor at the University of Maryland. The rise in drug use and smuggling has strained Iran's police forces and prisons, as well as its economy, and aggravated rifts along the population's main fault lines: young versus old, religious versus secular, modernist versus traditional. Drug abuse . . . if left unchecked . . . may leave Iran with large social, demographic, and health problems for generations.

Lionel Beehner, "Afghanistan's Role in Iran's Drug Problem,"
Council on Foreign Relations, September 14, 2006. wwww.cfr.org.

words, the AIDS epidemic has done nothing to open the way for treatment with methadone or any other treatment for heroin addiction" in the United States, Newman said.

Heroin Addiction Is Rising

In Iran, heroin addiction is rising in a population of drug users estimated at between 2 million and 4 million. Heroin use rose abruptly about five years ago [in 2000], when the Taliban rulers in neighboring Afghanistan sharply reduced opium production. That drove up the price of opium, leading people who had been smoking or swallowing it to switch to heroin, which remained comparatively cheap.

Because heroin is often injected, the switch resulted in a surge of HIV infections as users shared needles.

Until recently, the HIV infection rate among intravenous drug users in Iran had been estimated at 5 percent. But in blood tests of 900 users over eight months, the Persepolis clinic headed by Nasirimanesh found a rate of 25 percent. "The bomb exploded," he said.

Officials said that rate was confirmed by a more recent study conducted through Japan's Kyoto University. A lower rate, about 13 percent, was recorded among users who get their methadone at the addiction studies treatment center. Mokri said that was presumably because the center's clients are typically better off than the often homeless junkies at the Persepolis drop-in center and have avoided time in prisons where dirty needles are far more common.

But the rates in all surveys are headed up. "The potential is very bad," said Arbitrio of the U.N. agency. "If you have 160,000 injecting plus 3 million drug users, you have all the elements to have the spread of HIV/AIDS very quickly."

How quickly the virus might reach into the general population via sexual contact is a sensitive issue in Iran. Experts here do not see transmission though gay sex as an important avenue, but fear HIV will spread in a big way through heterosexual sex.

Though the government has promoted a puritanical view on premarital sex, it has tolerated prostitutes, who by many accounts have risen sharply in numbers in recent years.

"Before, Iran always said this is something from outside. Now they are accepting this is not only for drug users, but growing among people who are sexually active."

"I know some who are drug addicts," said Sorraya Heidari, 39, as she waited for methadone at the Persepolis clinic. "To get the money they need for drugs, they have to work as prostitutes."

There is also evidence that young people—half of Iran's population is under age 20—are more sexually active than some researchers believed. Fully 70 percent of capital residents ages 15 to 20 have had sex outside marriage, and almost none reported using condoms, according to a survey of 2,000 Tehran young people by Tehran University and the State Welfare Organization.

"Before, Iran always said this is something from outside," said Hamid Reza Setayesh, the UNAIDS officer for Iran. "Now they are accepting this is not only for drug users, but growing among people who are sexually active."

Experts say the official reluctance to promote condom use generally is a major drawback in Iran's evolving policy toward AIDS. Another is the lack of anonymous testing for the virus. "They ask for your name," Setayesh said. "And they should not ask."

Public health specialists also caution that many of the new policies have yet to be launched on a large scale. "The policies are very good," said Gelareh Mostashari, a physician in the U.N. drugs office. "But there are practical applications that have to be executed."

Still, many drug experts say the government has shown a consistent disregard for orthodoxies in this fight. Mokri said he was astonished to encounter no official resistance when he set out to launch a pilot program that will dispense actual opium instead of methadone to addicts.

He noted a bill pending in the U.S. Congress calling for imprisoning Americans who failed to report marijuana dealers. "Sometimes I think the ayatollahs are more liberal," Mokri said.

In Russia, Competing Moralities Hamper the Fight Against AIDS

Jarrett Zigon

Jarrett Zigon is an anthropology professor at the University of Amsterdam. In the following viewpoint, he argues that in Russia the two main institutions fighting the growing AIDS crisis are the Russian Orthodox Church (ROC) and secular nongovernmental organizations. He says these institutions advance different moralities. The Russian Orthodox Church, he argues, sees AIDS as the result of individual and societal moral breakdown. Secular care providers, he says, see nonjudgmental help for those at risk of AIDS as a moral human right. He concludes that these different moral visions make it hard for secular and religious groups to work together against AIDS. This article has been edited and adapted to suit this publication.

As you read, consider the following questions:

1. According to UNAIDS/WHO, how many cases of AIDS are there in Russia?
2. According to Zigon, what does *nravstvennost* entail?
3. Why did the NGO that Zigon discusses cut the number of needles it would exchange for an individual to one hundred per visit?

Adapted from Jarrett Zigon, "Morality and HIV/AIDS: A Comparison of Russian Orthodox Church and Secular NGO Approaches," *Religion, State and Society*, vol. 37, no. 3, September 2009, pp. 311, 314–323. Copyright © 2009 by Taylor & Francis. Reproduced by permission.

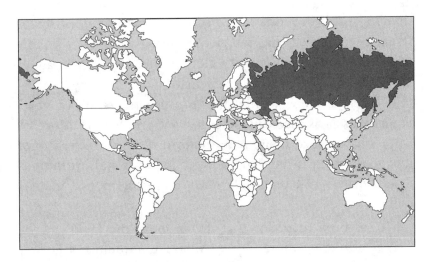

Russia now has the highest number of HIV-positive persons in Europe, and, according to a 2001 report by UN-AIDS (the Joint United Nations Programme on HIV/AIDS), one of the fastest HIV growth rates in the world. Yet prevention and treatment programmes remain scarce and underfunded. What programmes do exist can be seen as representing competing moral positions in the struggle against the HIV/AIDS crisis in Russia. This [viewpoint] is an attempt to disclose the moral assumptions behind the HIV prevention programmes offered by, on the one hand, the Russian Orthodox Church, and on the other, secular NGOs [nongovernmental organizations], and to consider how these assumptions influence the kinds of programmes offered. This will be done by comparing and contrasting the moral discourse and practices of each of these institutions and by providing examples from my fieldwork in St Petersburg. . . .

Moral Breakdown in Russia

For nearly the last 20 years [since the fall of Communism in 1989] the Russian people have been living through a period of social and political upheaval and cultural and epistemological [studying the nature and limits of human knowledge] questioning—or what is often referred to as a period of transition. It has been argued that rather than bringing about a condition of increased homogeneity, globalisation has brought about an 'increasing intensity of problematization'. It is my contention that like globalisation, the so-called transition of post-Soviet Russia is also characterised by problematisation, or what I have called above a breakdown. One characteristic of this questioning is the struggle by individuals and institutions to articulate a coherent and widely acceptable notion of morality.

It has been suggested that Russia today can be characterised as having no moral limits. Although I would not go this far, it is clear that Russia is characterised by the constant questioning of a moral breakdown, part of which consists of the struggle over competing moral conceptualisations. Thus, for example, Michele Rivkin-Fish argues that the Soviet-era concepts of *kul'turnost'* (culturedness) and *lichnost'* (individuality/person) are still used in the post-Soviet sphere of public health, where medical personnel use these tropes for the purpose of disciplining their patients to live healthier lifestyles or practise safe sex. Similarly, Rogers argues that the context of socio-political transition in the post-Soviet years has allowed for the renewal of 'conversations and conflicts about how to constitute moral relations', and Nancy Ries has shown how everyday forms and genres of speech are vital to the constitution of these moral relations. Thus, an obvious conclusion to be drawn from these works is that ethical work and moral transformation are possible because of the very differences that already exist between persons and institutions.

Such differences are seen quite explicitly in the debate over morality in the current HIV/AIDS crisis in Russia. Not only is this crisis the focal point of the contested moral visions of various institutions, but many Russians consider its cause to be a perceived general societal breakdown of morality. Therefore, I have chosen this topic not only because it is a topic of some importance and immediacy in Russia today, but also because it is an example of what I have called a moral breakdown. Thus the HIV/AIDS epidemic is the locus of, for example, debates about morality between the Russian Orthodox Church, secular NGOS and the Russian government; differing legislative, medical and support practices arising from this debate; and moral questioning both on the part of those who try to provide help and those who are receiving help. Furthermore, because the HIV/AIDS epidemic in Russia is driven by injecting-drug use, much of the prevention programme focus is on behavior change (it should be noted that even needle-exchange programmes are essentially behaviour change programmes, since their success depends upon injecting-drug users changing their previous behaviour of used-needle use to that of exchange and use of clean needles). These prevention programmes, as I shall show below, are thus examples of restitutions engaged in projects promoting ethical activity. . . . For this reason, then, the HIV/AIDS epidemic in Russia is an example of a moral breakdown and provides an opportunity for a focused anthropological study of moralities. . . .

It is clear that Russia is characterised by the constant questioning of a moral breakdown.

The Approach of the Russian Orthodox Church

Since 2001 Russia and Eastern Europe have had the unsettling distinction of having one of the fastest-growing HIV/AIDS epidemics in the world. As of December 2007 there have been over 400,000 officially registered cases of PLWHA [persons living with HIV/AIDS] in Russia. This number of registered cases ranks highest among all European countries and accounts for 70 per cent of reported cases in Eastern Europe and Central Asia. Outside official statements by the government, however, it is almost unanimously agreed that the number is much higher. According to one estimate, it could be as high as 1.4 million. However, most tend to reference the UNAIDS/WHO [World Health Organization] estimate of 940,000.

Russia differs significantly from most other countries in how the epidemic is spreading. In Africa, for example, the vast majority of the 27 million infected people became so through sex. Conversely, in Russia an estimated 70–80 per cent of PL-WHA became infected through the sharing of contaminated needles. Thus the Russian context differs significantly from the other epidemic 'hot spots' in terms of risk-groups, strategies for prevention and education. For this reason, my research focuses on injection-drug users as both a risk group and as individuals living with HIV/AIDS, and the ways in which these individuals are offered and seek help from the two organizations ... with which I did research: the Russian Orthodox Church and a local secular NGO.

Because the Russian government has done little but send mixed messages about its response to the HIV/AIDS crisis in the country, and provide inadequate funding for prevention and treatment, the bulk of the work in these areas has been taken up by nongovernmental organisations and the Russian Orthodox Church. In the rest of this [viewpoint] I will consider how these two institutions have taken part in this struggle and how their respective moral assumptions play a significant role in the services they provide and their inability to work together.

The ROC primarily sees this struggle as a battle for the moral rectification of the Russian nation.

The Russian Orthodox Church (ROC) is a latecomer to the world of HIV/AIDS prevention, treatment, policy advising and counselling. Indeed, it was not until October 2004 that the Holy Synod of the ROC approved *The Concept of the Rus-*

sian Orthodox Church's Participation in Overcoming the Spreading of HIV/AIDS and Work with People Living with HIV/AIDS (Kontseptsii, 2005). While this document states that the ROC is prepared to work in partnership with the state and what it calls society (civil society), it also makes it clear that the 'church does not consider it possible to collaborate with those public forces which by exploiting the theme of HIV/AIDS defend the way of life, behaviour and ethical views that are unacceptable to Christian morals'. As one church official stated at the public announcement of the document, the ROC will not make moral compromises in its efforts to fight the epidemic.

In fact, the ROC primarily sees this struggle as a battle for the moral rectification of the Russian nation. According to this document, the social and medical factors that many others see as the basis of the epidemic are secondary to the root cause of HIV/AIDS, which the ROC sees as 'the abundance of sin and lawlessness, and society's loss of fundamental spiritual values, moral foundations and orientation'. It is not surprising that the ROC sees sin and immorality as the basis of the propagation of HIV/AIDS. As one of the church officials who presented the document stated, 'society must not hide from the realisation that there is a connection between sin and the disease'. Nevertheless, the document explicitly states that HIV/AIDS should not be thought of as 'payback' for individual sins. Rather, it is the result of the sinful nature of humans. Thus the ROC's primary strategy for fighting the 'propagation of the HIV/AIDS epidemic is strengthening the spiritual and moral standards of society'. This is to be done through 'spiritual training'. . . .

The Approach of Secular NGOs

Unlike the ROC, which has only recently articulated its official concern about the HIV/AIDS epidemic, secular NGOs, both Russian and international, have been working on prevention, treatment, policy advising and counseling since the mid-1990s.

These organisations work at various levels and utilize different strategies in their struggle against the epidemic. While some of them work primarily with the Russian government and health agencies in order to achieve just laws and adequate medical attention for PLWHA, many other organisations work at street level, educating and treating both infected and at-risk individuals. It is impossible, then, to speak of these secular NGOs as united in their approaches, activities or assumptions. Nevertheless, it is possible to discern a general moral discourse that emerges through their various public documents.

The most obvious moral position taken by these NGOs is that the only way to combat the epidemic effectively is by guaranteeing human rights. These rights are seen as a way of empowering, on the one hand, PLWHA to participate in fighting the epidemic, and on the other hand, the population at large to avoid infection. Both the ROC and the secular NGOs refer to human nature; but the former stresses the need to reconcile it with Christian morality and the latter the need to empower it through human rights.

One key aspect to the secular NGO approach is to overcome 'moral objections' to prevention: in other words, to replace one moral approach with another. Instead of being stigmatised, drug users and sex workers should be given clean needles, condoms and information. The sexuality of young people should not simply be ignored, and sex education should be provided in schools rather than the teaching of Christian morality and family values. The moral and religious values underpinning censorship should be reconsidered in light of the potential benefit censored information could bring to fighting the epidemic. It would thus seem that one of the unstated goals of secular NGOs is to overcome a traditional morality that may hold some responsibility for the propagation of the epidemic and to replace it with another.

For the secular NGOs and the ROC alike, then, stopping the propagation of HIV/AIDS in Russia depends on a moral

HIV/AIDS Estimates for Russia

Population Characteristic	Figures for Russia
Total population	139.4 million (mid-2010)
Estimated population living with HIV/AIDS	940,000 [630,000–1,300,000] (end 2007)
Adult HIV prevalence	1.1% [0.8–1.6%] (end 2007)

HIV prevalence in most-at-risk populations	IDUs:
	  15.6% (National) (2009)
	  61.2% (St. Petersburg) (2009)
	MSM: [Men who have sex with men]
	  8.3% (National) (2009)
	  0.9% (Moscow) (2006)
	Sex workers:
	  15.6% (National) (2007)
	  4.5% (Moscow) (2009)
	  19.6% (Irkutsk) (2009)

Percentage of HIV-infected people receiving antiretroviral therapy	16% (end 2007)

TAKEN FROM: USAID, *Russia: HIV/AIDS Health Profile*, September 2010. http://www.usaid.gov.

overhaul, and they agree that the current moral standards prevailing in Russia are, if not the root cause of the epidemic, then certainly an impediment to overcoming it. The problem, however, is that they do not agree about the content of the desired morality. . . .

The moralities expressed in their discourse by these two institutions are clearly different. While the ROC is focused on a morality of behavior change, the NGO [in St. Petersburg at which the author did research] is more concerned with providing human rights. But what does this difference entail in practice? To consider this question I shall take a closer look at two of my research sites.

Two Moralities

The church-run rehabilitation centre [in St. Petersburg] has on average 25 rehabilitants at any one time, usually with equal numbers of males and females. Participants stay between three and four months. There are four staff members: an Orthodox priest, who is the leader of the centre; an Orthodox deacon; and two former drug users who underwent rehabilitation at the centre. The rehabilitation process combines what is called labour therapy, which consists basically of maintaining the farm at which the centre is located; religious practice, such as prayer and confession; religious education; and psychological and art therapy. Each of these practices is seen as an essential aspect of the moral training at the heart of the rehabilitation process.

The most obvious moral position taken by these NGOs is that the only way to combat the epidemic effectively is by guaranteeing human rights.

The Russian word used by the church and its staff members concerning the moral focus of their rehabilitation and HIV prevention and treatment programmes is *nravstvennost'*, which is etymologically related to both *nravy*, meaning way of life or customs, and *nrav*, which means disposition. Thus the moral focus of the church-run programme is twofold: (1) to train the person in a certain way of social being that is recognised as morally acceptable; and (2) to do this in such a way that the person comes to embody in an unreflective way this new moral way of being. *Nravstvennost'*, then, entails what I called above both morality and ethics. It is a way of working on oneself so as to become a socially acceptable person.

This *nravstvennost'* is acquired by means of the various therapies and religious practices performed at the rehabilitation centre. Thus, for example, by keeping to a very strict schedule, which begins at seven in the morning and ends at midnight, the rehabilitants are said to learn responsibility and motivation and to develop a sense of structure to their day. They also learn that prayer can be used as a way to push away immoral desires and temptations, such as drug use, fornication and anger, and they are encouraged to use prayer as often as possible so that it becomes a regular part of their lives.

Labour is a central aspect of the therapeutic and ethical training process at the rehabilitation centre. What is often referred to as labour therapy is considered preparation for living what is called a normal life (*normal'naya zhizn'*), that is, a life that includes a full-time job, a family and participation in the church. Labour therapy, then, is in a sense considered a kind of life and career training. In fact, many of the rehabilitants who returned to the city and with whom I was able to remain in contact found jobs closely related to the skills they learned at the centre—several became repair men or construction workers, others became janitors, and others became mechanics and drivers. Work is also a time, as it is in monastic life, for contemplation of oneself, one's past and future, and one's relationship with God. Work, then, is also an important part of the work on the self (*rabota nad soboi*) that many told me was the main task of the rehabilitation centre. During the eight-hour day of work and work on the self, rehabilitants have much time to think about the life they have lived so far and the ways in which they want to change for the future, to pray, and to think about the discussions had or lessons taught during group activities. Thus, for example, one young woman told me she tries to think about the main lessons of the group activity from the night before while she works, another told me that she spends her work day thinking about the people in her life whom she has hurt and what she can do to make up for it, and a young man once told me he tries to pray each day while working and think about the meaning of the prayers. In each of these ways and others, then, labour therapy is also a therapy for labouring on the self, and an example of the ethical work necessary to embody a new morality at the church-run rehabilitation centre.

While staff, literature, and even rehabilitants at the church-run rehabilitation centre often talk about the moral work going on there, I never heard it mentioned at the joint programme harm reduction centre.

Meanwhile the NGO's joint programme with the infectious disease hospital provides needle exchange, condom distribution, HIV and other testing, psychological and social counselling, and seminars for mothers who are HIV positive on how to look after their children safely. . . . There are many days when no one comes to the joint programme to take advantage of their services and there are others when up to ten will come. There are very few who could be called regulars.

While staff, literature and even rehabilitants at the church-run rehabilitation centre often talk about the moral work going on there, I never heard it mentioned at the joint programme harm reduction centre. In fact, when I first told the doctor who runs the programme about my research focus on moral approaches, he told me that 'we have no moral approach'. When I followed up on this question he was quick to acknowledge that human rights are, however, central to what the programme provides. While the doctor may not have drawn a connection between human rights and morality, a social worker who was in the room joined our conversation. 'Yes,' she told me, 'we provide a place where they [injecting drug users and PLWHA] can have their human rights. It is the most moral thing we can do.' What are these human rights provided by the joint programme?

According to one of the main HIV-prevention NGOs in Russia working on the issue of human rights for PLWHA and persons at risk, these rights consist of 'the right to the best attainable standard of physical and mental health; the right to access to information and education; the right to privacy; and the right to participate in scientific progress and enjoy its benefits'. Each of these rights is provided by the joint programme. For example, one of the main services offered at the joint programme is to provide free baby formula and safe care education for mothers who are HIV positive. This service consists of weekly seminars to teach HIV-positive mothers how to prevent transmission to their children and how to use the baby formula, as well as other more general child raising issues.

The needle-exchange service at the joint programme is also viewed as a human right, for it allows access to the latest scientific progress and information, it respects the privacy of those who exchange, and it includes informal moments of education on the safest methods of injecting heroin. The number of needles that can be exchanged per person was recently limited to 100 per visit. This was done because previously people would exchange as many as 1,000, bringing in the needles of their friends. With the change of policy the joint programme hoped that more people would come to exchange their own needles, and that they could thus be introduced to the services and rights provided by the programme. So far, however, the increase in clients has been minimal. . . .

We can see, then, a clear distinction between the two moral approaches of these institutions. While the ROC *nravstvennost'* approach focuses on the individual ethically working on himself or herself in order to become a 'normal person', the joint programme seeks to provide a moral world of safety, support and acceptance where injecting-drug users and PLWHA can come and find their human rights recognised. There is, of course, no doubt that the rehabilitants at the church-run centre also find their context safe, supportive and without stigma, and that participants in the joint programme are encouraged to alter their behaviour in some ways. Nevertheless, neither of these is the main focus of the moral approach of the respective programmes. They are, as it were, the background benefits of programmes that highlight the *other* moral approach. For whether the main moral focus is *nravstvennost'* or human rights, each institution understands, to a degree, the benefits of the other approach. . . .

These two institutions argue that the only thing that can stop the HIV/AIDS epidemic is a further and more complete realisation of the moral vision they espouse.

Talking Past One Another

In a social context where this epidemic is widely seen as a result of a society-wide moral breakdown, it should not be surprising that moral assumptions stand at the foundation of available prevention and treatment programmes. While there is some evidence that the kinds of harm reduction programmes offered by the joint programme and other NGOs in Russia are having some success in stemming the spread of the epidemic, and the ROC drug rehabilitation programmes report a 25 per cent success rate, the number of persons in Russia infected with HIV increases each year. So one must ask the eternal Russian question: What is to be done?

These two institutions argue that the only thing that can stop the HIV/AIDS epidemic is a further and more complete realisation of the moral vision they espouse. It is no wonder, then, that as the seminar at the HIV/AIDS conference in Moscow showed well, these two institutions are much more adept at speaking past one another than with one another. In such a situation where the two main institutions working on the HIV/AIDS crisis are unable to communicate with one another (in fact, nearly every time I told NGO staff workers that I was also working with the Russian Orthodox Church they responded that they did not think the ROC was doing anything on this issue), and the government does little more than provide mixed messages about the extent of the crisis and inadequate funding, it is little wonder that the number of HIV cases continues to grow. It seems, then, that the HIV epidemic in Russia is not only a medical and social problem, but also a problem of moral interpretation and understanding; and therefore that neither of these institutions will have much further success without first either dropping their moral agenda, which appears unlikely, or learning how to integrate the other moral approach into their own. For only in this way will these two institutions begin to cooperate rather than speak past one another, and in so doing, learn from and build on the successes and failures of each other.

The Pope's Opposition to Condom Use Is Moral

Timothy Finigan

Timothy Finigan is a Catholic priest at the parish of Our Lady of the Rosary, Blackfen, in Kent, United Kingdom. In the following viewpoint he argues that Catholicism teaches that sexual activity should occur only for the purposes of procreation. Therefore, he says, condom use is not an acceptable response to AIDS. In fact, nations that have focused on abstinence, like the Philippines and Uganda, have had the most success in fighting AIDS. Those that have focused on condom distribution, like Thailand, have been less successful. He adds that Britain's reliance on condom usage and sex education has only increased the incidence of sexually transmitted infections (STIs). He concludes that the pope's focus on abstinence is moral.

As you read, consider the following questions:

1. At what point does Finigan say that it became controversial to claim that sexual thoughts, words, or actions deliberately indulged in outside marriage were sinful?
2. According to Finigan, how many AIDS cases were there in 2003 in Thailand and the Philippines respectively?
3. Between 1995 and 2004, what were the percentage changes in syphilis, gonorrhea, and other STIs in Britain, according to the author?

Timothy Finigan, "AIDS, Condoms and the Catholic Church," *Our Lady of the Rosary*, 2006. Copyright © 2006 by Rev. Timothy Finigan. Reproduced by permission.

I wish to begin by saying very clearly that the global incidence of infection with HIV and the effects of the virus in AIDS with consequent illness and, in many cases around the world, premature death, is a cause for sorrow among Catholics, Christians and indeed all people of good will.

HIV, Homosexuality and the Church

As I will outline later, the Church's response has been vigorous in many places throughout the world with dedicated people looking after those who are living with HIV and AIDS. Nor is such caring work simply the work of a few charismatic individuals, it is very much encouraged at the highest official level within the Catholic Church.

The Catholic Church is active in working to alleviate suffering of many different kinds. From the example of our Lord himself, we have always sought out those who were outcast. In the time of Jesus it was the lepers who were signally excluded from the community. Following the example of Jesus, we find heroic stories of people such as St Francis and Blessed Damien of Molokai who worked among lepers and brought to them a renewed sense of their human dignity.

This may be obvious to some of you but I want to say it clearly at the outset because in my experience, the misrepresentation of the work of the Church is sometimes breathtaking and we cannot necessarily assume that people know the truth.

Unfortunately, HIV and AIDS have assumed a particular political importance because of two factors. The first is that in Western countries, HIV and AIDS have been associated, rightly or wrongly, with homosexual activity. On the one hand, homosexuals have campaigned against AIDS being seen as a "gay plague." On the other hand, homosexuals have campaigned against the stigma attached to HIV and AIDS—partly because in the West, homosexuals have been over-represented among those who have been infected with the virus.

At the same time, we have seen in the past twenty years a growing political "gay" movement which has sought to promote homosexual behaviour as one of many acceptable lifestyles. Allied with this is the growth in many of our cities of gay bars, gay areas, gay publications and now public advertising specifically targeted at the "gay pound."

The Catholic Church is active in working to alleviate suffering of many different kinds.

The second factor which is related to the first is the growth of the assumption in the West that sexual activity should not be regulated in any way and that people have the right, from an early age, to engage in sexual activity as they see fit, provided that there is no coercion involved. Therefore, whatever response is made to the incidence of infection with HIV, there is considerable resistance to the idea of abstinence.

The Catholic Church has responded to both of these currents of thought.

On the question of sexual licence, the Catholic Church has always taught and continues to teach that sexual activity has a built-in meaning. It is intended by the creator for the procreation of children within the context of marriage. Outside of this context, any sexual thought, word or action, deliberately indulged, is sinful. Until earlier in this century, this teaching was uncontroversial and was shared by all Christians, Jews, Muslims, people of other faiths and by most non-believers.

This teaching is found clearly set out in the *Catechism of the Catholic Church*. The *Catechism* also summarises how the same teaching applies to the particular case of homosexual acts. However, after explaining this with reference to scripture, it goes on:

The number of men and women who have deep-seated homosexual tendencies is not negligible. This inclination, which is objectively disordered, constitutes for most of them a trial. They must be accepted with respect, compassion, and sensitivity. Every sign of unjust discrimination in their regard should be avoided. These persons are called to fulfill God's will in their lives and, if they are Christians, to unite to the sacrifice of the Lord's Cross the difficulties they may encounter from their condition.

Homosexual persons are called to chastity. By the virtues of self-mastery that teach them inner freedom, at times by the support of disinterested friendship, by prayer and sacramental grace, they can and should gradually and resolutely approach Christian perfection.

This teaching is a perfectly reasonable approach to the question from the point of view of scripture and the Christian tradition, and indeed is more compassionate than the views which most people would have held only a few years ago. Nevertheless, it is now a dangerous teaching to promote. It is characterised as "homophobic" and anyone publicly promoting this Catholic teaching is increasingly likely to be subjected to abuse. . . .

The Catholic Church has always taught and continues to teach that sexual activity. . . . is intended by the creator for the procreation of children within the context of marriage.

What Actually Works?

I will begin by looking at the facts related to the worldwide epidemic of HIV/AIDS.

HLI [Human Life International] published an interesting article comparing the Philippines and Thailand. I believe that it is instructive in this debate. What follows is an edited version of the article, which includes the statistics but omits some of the comments on them.

The first AIDS cases were diagnosed in both Thailand and the Philippines in 1984. By 1987, there were 112 cases of HIV/AIDS infection in Thailand and 135 cases in the Philippines.

In 1991 the World Health Organization (WHO) AIDS Program forecasted that by 1999 Thailand would have 60,000 to 80,000 cases, and that the Philippines would experience between 80,000 and 90,000 cases of HIV/AIDS.

In Thailand, the Minister of [Public] Health launched the "100% Condom Use Program." All brothels were required to stock a large supply of condoms, and condom vending machines appeared in supermarkets, bars and other public places.

In 1992, the Philippines' Secretary of Health (now a senator), Mr. Juan Flavier, tried to implement the program in the Philippines. However, the programme was not adopted because of popular opposition. In 1999 the UNAIDS [Joint United Nations Programme on HIV/AIDS] reported 755,000 total confirmed cases of HIV infection in Thailand—65,000 had died of the disease. That same year, in the Philippines, the total number of HIV cases was only 1,005. The disease had killed only 225 people.

As of August 2003 there were 899,000 HIV/AIDS cases documented in Thailand and approximately 125,000 deaths attributed to the disease. These numbers are many times those projected by the WHO (60,000–80,000 cases) in 1991.

It does not give any credit for the public policy in the Philippines promoting abstinence, monogamy and faithfulness.

These numbers contrast sharply with those of the Philippines where, as of September 30, 2003, there were 1,946 AIDS cases resulting in 260 deaths. This is only a mere fraction of the number of cases (80,000–90,000) that the WHO projected would be reached by 2000.

Incidentally, Thailand has a smaller population (66 million) than the Philippines (82 million).

The UNAIDS Epidemic Update 2004 recognises that Thailand is among those countries that has an "extremely low" level of HIV prevalence. It does not give any credit for the public policy in the Philippines promoting abstinence, monogamy and faithfulness but continues to say that such countries have a golden opportunity to pre-empt a serious outbreak.

Uganda and Botswana

In an article written for the University of [Kwazulu-]Natal's [Health Economics and HIV/AIDS Research Division, or HEARD], [Jeremy] Liebowitz shows that in Uganda, there was all overall decline in average infection rates across the country from 14% to 8.3% between 1993 and 1999. The reduction in HIV prevalence was also recognised by the UNAIDS Epidemic update in 2002.

Liebowitz showed that the principal cause of this reduction is changes in sexual behaviour, influenced greatly by "faith-based organizations" who have encouraged fidelity, abstinence and remaining with one partner.

A Harvard [University] study found that when the abstinence promotion programme in Uganda began, in the late 1980s, the number of pregnant women infected with HIV was 21.2 percent. By 2001, the number was 6.2 percent. The study also found that women 15 and older who had many sexual partners dropped from 18.4 percent in 1989 to 2.5 percent in 2000. (The abstinence programme was given the name "True Love Waits.")

Among secular researchers, it is recognised that faith-based strategies are more successful in Uganda because they promote more culturally appropriate solutions. Interestingly, it is also noted that the stigmatization of people with HIV/AIDS has lowered at the same time. Liebowitz also notes that the

Catholic Church in particular has been successful in reaching out to those suffering with HIV/AIDS because of its teaching on Christian charity and acceptance of and care for AIDS sufferers. He also found that the Catholic Church is better mobilised to help because of its network of health care facilities.

In Botswana, by contrast, where condom use is promoted heavily, 38% of pregnant women were HIV positive in 2001 compared with 6.2% in Uganda.

Among secular researchers, it is recognised that faith-based strategies are more successful in Uganda because they promote more culturally appropriate solutions.

In Kenya, there has been a fierce debate over the promotion of condoms. One voice in this debate was Sheikh Khalif, secretary general of the Supreme Council of Kenyan Muslims, who said:

Muslims are opposed to the use of condoms for this will boost promiscuity. We cannot bend God's laws to make them conform to the passions of man.

As the *Daily Nation* remarked, there was no framing of this response in the usual terms of a church-state standoff that characterises coverage of similar comments by Christian leaders.

Publicly, the issue of promoting condoms has been so controversial in Kenya that there was even an outbreak among young people of "condom burning" because they saw the promotion of condoms as clearly harmful to society.

Senegal is another case in point. It has successfully maintained an HIV prevalence rate of below 2%. The local religious leaders ("marabouts") have effectively encouraged their followers to behave in a morally good way in the use of sex. Liebowitz acknowledges:

... encouragement of abstinence by a *marabout* may prove a more effective deterrent than commands to use condoms from a district health official.

The English sex-education policy has been a disastrous failure with England now having the highest teenage pregnancy rate in Europe.

England and Sex Education

We can see a strong parallel between the promotion of condoms as a preventive measure against HIV infection and the promotion of contraception in England as a means of reducing teenage pregnancy.

The English sex-education policy has been a disastrous failure with England now having the highest teenage pregnancy rate in Europe. Yet the Teenage Pregnancy Unit on the home page of its website directs young people to the Brook, Sexwise, Marie Stopes [International], the British Pregnancy Advisory Service and the Family Planning Association, all of which promote contraception as a major strategy in dealing with the problem of teenage pregnancy and all of which support abortion as an option.

The Health Protection Agency statistics make depressing reading. The percentage change from 1995–2004 shows large increases in syphilis (1449%), gonorrhea (111%), chlamydia (223%), herpes (15%) and genital warts (32%). The 2003 report to the Select Committee on Health summarised it well by saying that "the last decade has witnessed a dramatic rise in diagnoses of all major [sexually transmitted] diseases." In 2000, the Office for National Statistics did a report showing data on the use of condoms in the previous four weeks. It found that 46% of males and 37% of females with one or more new partners used condoms on every occasion that they had sex.

If you have been given the impression that if you wear a condom, you are safe from STIs, you need to consider those figures.

By the way, you also need to know that on its sexual health myths and facts page, Bupa [a British health care company] lists as "Myth 3" the statement "Condoms protect against all STIs". I quote:

> [...] according to the Family Planning Association, there is little evidence to suggest that condoms protect against the transmission of genital warts. It is also uncertain whether or not condoms can protect against genital herpes.

This is not some Catholic thing, it is publically available information. But when were you ever told? Furthermore, it is recognised that genital herpes, for example, is not curable. If you have it, you have it for life. So will your sexual partner(s).

Let us consider again those figures from the Health Protection Agency. Which of the diseases were condoms supposed to protect against? These infections and others not listed put you at risk, variously, of infertility, pelvic inflammatory disease, cervical cancer—oh, and of course, premature death. Marie Stopes has a sex-ed website for children called "likeitis" which calls these infections "Love Bugs".

In England this dramatic rise in STIs (also in teenage pregnancies and abortions) has taken place against the backdrop of the "more and better sex education" mantra. The message seems to be "it has dismally failed so far so let's keep on trying the same thing".

If we were to learn from Uganda and the Philippines, we would promote chastity education and the ideal of one partner for life as an achievable and fulfilling goal. Quite clearly, the promotion of contraception encourages an increase in sexual activity, whether among the young, whether in England or in Africa. The promotion of chastity, one partner for life, fidelity and responsibility are exactly what the Catholic Church teaches. It is not Pope John Paul who is responsible for millions of deaths in Africa.

The Pope's Opposition to Condom Use Is Immoral

Ben Goldacre

Ben Goldacre is a psychiatrist, a science writer for the Guardian, *and the author of the book* Bad Science. *In the following viewpoint, he argues that condoms are an effective method of preventing the spread of AIDS. He points out that the pope and Catholic bishops have actively campaigned against condom use. They have also, he says, repeatedly misrepresented the efficacy of condoms in preventing the spread of AIDS. He concludes that the church's campaign against condom use, especially in Africa, contributes to the AIDS crisis and is immoral.*

As you read, consider the following questions:

1. According to Goldacre, what percentage of the population is HIV positive in Botswana, Swaziland, Namibia, and Lesotho?
2. Why did Cardinal Alfonso López Trujillo of Columbia say that condoms were ineffective?
3. What does Goldacre say the acronym ABC stands for?

This week [September 2010] the pope is in London. You will have your own views on the discrimination against women, the homophobia, and the international criminal conspiracy to cover up for mass child rape [worldwide, many Catholic priests have been found to have sexually abused children]. My special interest is his role in the 2 million people who die of AIDS each year.

Pope Benedict XVI explained that AIDS is a tragedy "that cannot be overcome through the distribution of condoms, which even aggravates the problems".

First Pronouncement on AIDS

In May 2005, shortly after taking office, the pope [Pope Benedict XVI] made his first pronouncement on AIDS, and came out against condoms. He was addressing bishops from South Africa, where somebody dies of AIDS every two minutes; Botswana, where 23.9% of adults between 15 and 49 are HIV positive; Swaziland, where 26.1% of adults have HIV; Namibia (a trifling 15%); and Lesotho, 23%.

This is continuing. In March 2009, on his flight to Cameroon (where 540,000 people have HIV), Pope Benedict XVI explained that AIDS is a tragedy "that cannot be overcome through the distribution of condoms, which even aggravates the problems". In May 2009, the Congolese bishops conference made a happy announcement: "In all truth, the pope's message which we received with joy has confirmed us in our fight against HIV/AIDS. We say no to condoms!"

His stance has been supported, in the past year alone, by Cardinal George Pell of Sydney and Cardinal Cormac Murphy O'Connor, the Archbishop of Westminster. "It is quite ridiculous to go on about AIDS in Africa and condoms, and the Catholic Church," says O'Connor.

"I talk to priests who say, 'My diocese is flooded with condoms and there is more AIDS because of them.'"

Some have been more imaginative in their quest to spread the message against condoms. In 2007, Archbishop Francisco

Chimoio of Mozambique announced that European condom manufacturers are deliberately infecting condoms with HIV to spread AIDS in Africa. Out of every 8 people in Mozambique, one has HIV.

It was Cardinal Alfonso López Trujillo of Colombia who most famously claimed that the HIV virus can pass through tiny holes in the rubber of condoms. Again, he was not alone. "The condom is a cork," said Bishop Demetrio Fernandez of Spain, "and not always effective."

In 2005 Bishop Elio Sgreccia, president of the Pontifical Academy for Life, explained that scientific research has never proven that condoms "immunise against infection".

Overall, rates of HIV infection were 80% lower in the partners who reported always using a condom, compared to those who said they never did. 80% is pretty good.

Condoms Stop the Virus

He's right, they don't. They stop the virus which kills you from being transmitted during sex.

How effective are they? It's wise not to overstate your case. The current systematic review of the literature on this question published by Cochrane [Collaboration] found 14 observational studies (because it's unethical to do a randomised trial where you actively stop people using condoms, since you know that they work but just want to find out how well).

These studies generally looked at HIV transmission in stable couples where one partner had HIV.

Many of them looked at transfusion patients and haemophiliacs. Overall, rates of HIV infection were 80% lower in the partners who reported always using a condom, compared to those who said they never did. 80% is pretty good.

There is no single perfect solution to the problem of AIDS: If things were that easy, it wouldn't be killing 2 million people every year.

Condoms Are Effective

Latex condoms, when used consistently and correctly, are highly effective in preventing heterosexual sexual transmission of HIV, the virus that causes AIDS. Research on the effectiveness of latex condoms in preventing heterosexual transmission is both comprehensive and conclusive. The ability of latex condoms to prevent transmission has been scientifically established in laboratory studies as well as in epidemiologic studies of uninfected persons at very high risk of infection because they were involved in sexual relationships with HIV-infected partners. The most recent meta-analysis of epidemiologic studies of condom effectiveness was published by Weller and Davis [Cochrane Reviews] in 2004. This analysis refines and updates their previous report published in 1999. The analysis demonstrates that the consistent use of latex condoms provides a high degree of protection against heterosexual transmission of HIV. It should be noted that condom use cannot provide absolute protection against HIV. The surest way to avoid transmission of HIV is to abstain from sexual intercourse or to be in a long-term mutually monogamous relationship with a partner who has been tested and you know is uninfected.

Centers for Disease Control and Prevention,
"Questions and Answers: HIV Prevention,"
October 20, 2006. www.cdc.gov.

ABC is a widely used prevention acronym in Africa: abstain, be [faithful], [use a] condom. Picking out one effective measure and actively campaigning against it is plainly destructive, just as telling people to abstain doesn't make everyone abstain, and telling people to use condoms won't make everyone use them. But Ratzinger [that is, Joseph Ratzinger, the

Pope] has proclaimed: "The most effective presence on the front in the battle against HIV/AIDS is the Catholic Church and her institutions."

This is ludicrous. You, the Catholic Church, [are] the only major influential international political organisation that actively tells people not to do something that works—on a huge scale. Your own figures show that your numbers are growing in Africa, even faster than the population does.

I'm happy for you to suggest abstention. But sabotaging an effective intervention which prevents a disease that kills 2 million people a year makes you a serious global public health problem.

Periodical and Internet Sources Bibliography

The following articles have been selected to supplement the diverse views presented in this chapter.

All China
Women's Federation

"China Appoints First Anti-AIDS Discrimination Ambassador," December 2, 2010. www.womenofchina.cn.

Daniel Blake

"Pope Promotes Morality Not Contraception in Africa AIDS Fight," *Christian Today*, March 18, 2009.

Canadian
AIDS Society

"Criminalization of HIV—Media Speaking Points," January 2009. www.cdnaids.ca.

CBS News

"Pope: Condom Use Can Be Justified to Halt AIDS," November 20, 2010.

Shannon Firth

"HIV a Murder Weapon in Canadian Court," *Finding Dulcinea*, April 8, 2009. www.finding dulcinea.com.

David Gibson

"The Catholic Church, Condoms, and 'Lesser Evils,'" *New York Times*, November 27, 2010.

Human Rights Watch

"Uganda: Bill Threatens Progress on HIV/AIDS," December 6, 2009. www.hrw.org.

Interfax

"Moscow Patriarchate Supports Position of Pope Benedict XVI Rejecting Condoms," March 20, 2009.

Tristana Moore

"In Germany, No Angels Star Faces HIV Charges," *Time*, April 16, 2009.

Karishma Vaswami

"Indonesia HIV-AIDS 'Spreading Through Sex,'" *BBC News*, December 1, 2009.

Matthew Weait

"Law Should Not Reinforce HIV Stigma," *Guardian* (UK), July 2, 2010.

CHAPTER 4

Discrimination and HIV/AIDS

HIV/AIDS Is Spreading Among Children in Eastern Europe Because of Discrimination

Nina Ferencic, Ruslan Malyuta, Paul Nary, and Jadranka Mimica

Nina Ferencic is senior advisor on HIV and AIDS in Central and Eastern Europe and the Commonwealth of Independent States for the United Nations Children's Fund (UNICEF); Ruslan Malyuta, Paul Nary, and Jadranka Mimica are all also UNICEF staff. In the following viewpoint, the authors note that Eastern Europe and Russia have a growing incidence of HIV. They argue that marginal populations affected by AIDS in Eastern Europe are often seen as immoral. As a result, the authors say, popular support for help is limited. They conclude that stigma and discrimination especially hurt young people with the disease.

As you read, consider the following questions:

1. According to the authors, what percentage of people living with HIV in the region are under thirty?

2. The authors say that the first reports of HIV/AIDS among children in the region came from where and involved what?

3. Why do the authors believe a political legacy of authoritarianism and control has made confronting HIV/AIDS difficult?

The story of the HIV epidemic in Eastern Europe and Central Asia is one of courage and commitment, but also of blame and banishment. Too often, those living with HIV have been silenced and excluded, and risky behaviours borne of futility and hopelessness have been sanctioned or repressed. As in other parts of the world, the shame and fear associated with AIDS have led to discrimination and denial, sometimes extreme. Evidence has been repressed, misconceptions rationalized, and the distress of those affected by HIV ignored. Although valuable national and local responses to HIV have been mounted, effective HIV treatment and prevention programmes have largely failed to reach those who are most vulnerable, in particular young people. The insidious consequence of this has been a hidden epidemic which disproportionately strikes young people, adolescents and children.

The central challenge of responding to HIV in most countries of the region is the need to come to terms with an epidemic that mostly affects people deemed by society to be 'delinquent' or 'anti-social'. Every day, children and young people engage in behaviours that put them at risk of HIV infection. In some cases, peer pressure, curiosity or just the natural recklessness of their age leads them to experiment with drugs or sexuality without thinking of the consequences. But many have been driven to the edge by social, economic and family problems. Few educational and employment opportunities, as well as weakening family and social support structures, have led to disillusionment and defiance in many young people, often expressed via increased risk-taking behaviour. Whatever the reasons, effective solutions cannot rest on social condemnation and exclusion.

Hope for the future lies in new models of integrated services for women, children and young people that are being developed by both civil society organizations and governments. Based on principles of respect and understanding, and focused on reducing risk and harm, these new service approaches are essential if children, young people and adults are to avoid being infected and if those living with HIV are to receive the support and care they need.

Care and compassion, not blame and banishment, must dictate how the realities of affected children and young people are addressed. Without greater solidarity and social acceptance, their suffering, often perceived as self-inflicted, falls into the moral gap between what is simply acknowledged and what constitutes an imperative to act.

This report is about changing that.

Care and compassion, not blame and banishment, must dictate how the realities of affected children and young people are addressed.

A Growing Epidemic Affecting Young People

Eastern Europe and Central Asia are the only parts of the world where the HIV epidemic remains clearly on the rise. Increases of up to 700 per cent in HIV infection rates have been found in some parts of the Russian Federation since 2006.[1] Over the past decade, there have also been important increases in HIV incidence in Central Asia and in the Caucasus, much of which remains under-reported.

The HIV epidemic in the region is driven by an explosive mix of injecting drug use and, more recently, sexual transmission. Children and young people, including those living on the streets, constitute a group whose risk of contracting HIV is particularly high. Today, one-third of new HIV infections in the region are among the 15–24 age group and more than 80 per cent of people living with HIV in the region are under 30 years old.[2]

The region is home to 3.7 million people who inject drugs, representing almost one-quarter of the world total. Some 1.8 million of these live in the Russian Federation and close to 300,000 each in Azerbaijan and in Ukraine.[3] The highest prevalence of injecting drug use in the adult population worldwide is now found in Azerbaijan (5.2 per cent), Georgia (4.2 per cent), Russian Federation (1.8 per cent) and Ukraine (1.2 per cent).[4]

Eastern Europe and Central Asia are the only parts of the world where the HIV epidemic remains clearly on the rise.

The average age of injecting drug users (IDUs) in the region is very low, with the age of initiating injecting still decreasing in a number of countries. In Moscow, Russian Federation, in 2005 the average age of injection start-up was 16 years old.[5] A UNICEF assessment in the former Yugoslav Republic of Macedonia found a growing number of 12- and 13-year-olds already using drugs.[6] Some 80 per cent of sex workers in Central and Eastern Europe are also young people, with female drug users often selling sex to support their drug use and that of their male partners.[5]

Women, who now account for some 40 per cent of new cases compared to just 24 per cent under a decade ago,[7,8] are increasingly affected by HIV, as are children. The total number of HIV-positive pregnancies has doubled during the past five years. Although rates of mother-to-child transmission of HIV have declined significantly as a result of effective implementation of national prevention of mother-to-child transmission (PMTCT) programmes, HIV infection still remains a signifi-

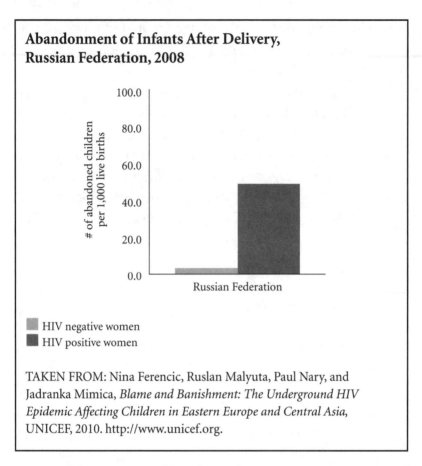

Abandonment of Infants After Delivery, Russian Federation, 2008

# of abandoned children per 1,000 live births

- HIV negative women
- HIV positive women

TAKEN FROM: Nina Ferencic, Ruslan Malyuta, Paul Nary, and Jadranka Mimica, *Blame and Banishment: The Underground HIV Epidemic Affecting Children in Eastern Europe and Central Asia,* UNICEF, 2010. http://www.unicef.org.

cant problem among drug-dependent pregnant women and their newborns, who tend to be missed by services.

Since 2006, there have been new reports of children contracting HIV in health settings due to unsafe injection practices, poor management of blood products and outdated clinical practices. As a result, 'outbreaks' of HIV infection among children have been confirmed in Kazakhstan, Kyrgyzstan and Uzbekistan.

Children and HIV in Context . . .

In Eastern Europe and Central Asia, most children infected through mother-to-child transmission have been diagnosed in the past five years. However, children have always been a prominent part of the epidemic in the region. The first reports on HIV/AIDS among children came in the early 1990s with the opening of post-Ceausescu Romania. The world was shocked by reports of HIV infections caused by untested blood and unsafe injections involving more than 10,000 children. But that was just the beginning....

The HIV epidemic became established in Eastern Europe and Central Asia in the mid-1990s, at a time of dramatic social and political change following the collapse of the Soviet Union. Two aspects of this historical and socio-economic context merit particular attention.

For some children from troubled families, the streets became their home or source of livelihood, and risk behaviours became a part of their daily lives.

Fragile Societies, Fragile Families

First, the effects of transition had a substantial impact both on individuals and the state. The transition left many states fragile. Ethnic conflicts erupted in a number of areas, including the Caucasus, Moldova, Tajikistan and the former Yugoslavia. In 1998, a major economic shock pushed the Russian Federation, and subsequently Ukraine, into deep recession. The 'colour revolutions' in Kyrgyzstan, Georgia, and Ukraine were visible manifestations of the political changes sweeping through the region. These events, combined with a focus on economic recovery, contributed to social issues, in particular those involving children, being pushed to the bottom of the agenda.

Recent improvements in household incomes across the region have masked widening gaps between those who have benefited from change and others who have been left behind. Social protection systems, which have rarely been high on regional reform agendas, have mostly not prioritized social assistance for families, community-based services, or child benefits. Levels of public health expenditure have remained extremely low in a number of countries. In principle, health services are meant to be universal and free of charge. In reality, however, these services have often been compromised, especially for the poor, by high informal payments and poor quality of service delivery.

Confronted with economic hardship, rising unemployment, social pressures and the crumbling of established social safety nets, many families found themselves unable to cope with the difficulties of socio-economic change and transition. These constraints, combined with widespread consumption of alcohol and drugs, reduced the capacity of many to protect their children. For some children from troubled families, the streets became their home or source of livelihood, and risk behaviours became a part of their daily lives. At their height, these street children were estimated to number a staggering one to four million.

Today, while there are no reliable estimates on the numbers of children on the streets, the vulnerabilities of children and families remain largely the same. The current economic and political crises in the region have revealed fragile foundations. According to the World Bank,[9] some 50.1 million people are now estimated to be living beneath the poverty line. Social reforms have stalled and social welfare budgets are being cut back.

A Difficult Political Inheritance

The second challenge of addressing the HIV epidemic in the region has been a political legacy of authoritarianism and control. Faced with an epidemic that mostly affects socially excluded populations such as drug users and sex workers, post-Soviet systems and mind-sets have found it difficult to tailor inclusive responses to meet the specific needs of marginalized groups and those living with HIV. Rigid social controls have often led to denunciation and blame of those who fail to conform, or who are caught up in systemic failures. In these circumstances, the stigma and discrimination related to fear and ignorance about HIV find reinforcement in official attitudes of intolerance, and in existing public prejudice against those whose behaviour is seen as 'anti-social' or 'immoral'. Children born to HIV-positive mothers suffer the consequences of these prejudices, experiencing a much higher likelihood than other children of being abandoned at a hospital, or being left to live in isolation at a specialized care institution.

Rigid social controls have often led to denunciation and blame of those who fail to conform, or who are caught up in systemic failures.

Negative attitudes and the denial of uncomfortable social realities lie at the root of children and young people's vulnerability to HIV infection and continue to be major barriers to addressing the real needs of children and their families. Policies and programmes remain strongly influenced by the legacy of the past and continue to ignore clear evidence about what constitutes an effective response as well as the everyday realities of those affected by HIV. As a result, opportunities for progress are being missed, allocation of resources often fails to match needs, and interventions may even aggravate the problems they are intended to alleviate.

Children and young people are being failed by this response.

References

1. Vitek C. Update on the epidemiology of the HIV epidemic in Eastern Europe and Central Asia presented at the Third Eastern European and Central Asian AIDS Conference, Moscow, October 2009.

2. WHO and UNAIDS. Progress on Implementing the Dublin Declaration on Partnership to Fight HIV/AIDS in Europe and Central Asia. Geneva, 2008.

3. Mathers B, et al. HIV prevention, treatment and care for people who inject drugs: a systematic review of global, regional and national coverage. *The Lancet*, 375(9719):1014–28, March 2010.

4. International Harm Reduction Association. The Global State of Harm Reduction 2010.

5. Eurasian Harm Reduction Network. Young people and injecting drug use in selected countries of Central and Eastern Europe. 2009, p. 30.

6. Stojanovik N, Dokuzovski D. The FYR of Macedonia: Most-at-risk Adolescents and Young People, HIV and Substance Use. UNICEF mission report. 2006.

7. UNAIDS. 2008 Report on the global AIDS epidemic. Geneva, 2008, p. 53.

8. UNAIDS. The changing HIV/AIDS epidemic in Europe and Central Asia. Geneva, 2004, p. 5.

9. Chen S, Ravallion M. The developing world is poorer than we thought, but no less successful in the fight against poverty. Policy Research Working Paper. World Bank. 2008.

HIV/AIDS Is Spreading in Eastern Europe Because of Free Market Changes

Markus Salzmann

Markus Salzmann is a reporter for the World Socialist Web Site. In the following viewpoint, he argues that the main cause of the spread of HIV/AIDS in Eastern Europe is not discrimination. Instead, he blames the crisis on the social chaos and breakdown caused by the too-rapid change from communism to capitalism. He notes that before the collapse of the Soviet Union, HIV/AIDS was not a serious problem in the region. He also argues that the problem has worsened as Western nations have cut aid money to the region.

As you read, consider the following questions:

1. According to Salzmann, by how much did HIV infections increase in some areas of Russia?

2. What does Salzmann say has led to two-tier health care in the region?

3. Why has Austria cut all its spending on HIV/AIDS abroad, according to Salzmann?

The rapid spread of HIV in Eastern Europe underscores the true scale of social devastation following the reintroduction of capitalism [in 1989] into the former Soviet Union and Eastern Europe.

The Effect on Children

An HIV epidemic is spreading rapidly in Eastern Europe and Central Asia, particularly among children and adolescents. UNICEF [United Nations Children's Fund] warned of these developments in a report published in mid-July [2010]. Nowhere else in the world is the rate of HIV infection climbing so rapidly as in this region.

The UN [United Nations] puts the number of those with HIV infection in Eastern Europe at 1.5 million; in 2001, the figure was 900,000. In some areas of Russia, the number of infections increased by 700 percent from 2006 to today. Over 90 percent of all infected people in this region can be found in Russia and Ukraine.

Those particularly affected are children and young people; and especially those who are living in abject poverty—children in care, drug addicts, street kids or underage prostitutes. Overall, one-third of new infections in the entire region are accounted for by youths and young adults, with 80 percent of those infected being younger than 30.

Another sign of social decline is the increasing drug use. The most common HIV transmission vector is contaminated needles, with many street kids already using hard drugs from the age of 12.

About 1.3 million children in the region are growing up in institutions where appalling conditions are the norm, and most soon end up on the streets.

A recent study in St. Petersburg found that among 300 street kids, 40 percent were HIV positive. Similarly high rates were found in Odessa and Donetsk in Ukraine. A survey conducted by UNICEF in Ukraine of 800 children and adolescents who spent half the day on the streets showed that 57 percent of girls engaged at least occasionally in prostitution.

Another sign of social decline is the increasing drug use. The most common HIV transmission vector is contaminated needles, with many street kids already using hard drugs from the age of 12.

The focus of the report and its criticism was the taboo with which HIV and AIDS are regarded. This is true of course. For example, in 2008, Turkmenistan officially reported only two cases of HIV infection—even though the epidemic had engulfed the country long ago.

Discrimination Is Secondary

But the real reason for the enormous spread of HIV/AIDS lies in the changing social and political conditions in these countries. The spread of the virus is directly related to the destruction of the health system and social infrastructure carried out at the beginning of the 1990s in the name of the free market.

"The spread of HIV started in the mid-1990s in the Ukraine and Belarus", according to Reinhard Kurth, who heads the Berlin Robert Koch Institute. It then quickly expanded to the north and east. In the meantime, Central Asia and the Caucasus are particularly affected by the pandemic.

An employee of the Austrian foreign ministry, who acts as a regional doctor in Moscow, points to a direct correlation between the spread of the virus and the social crisis in the East. In a statement, Dr. Wolfgang Luster writes, "Until the collapse of the Soviet Union, the countries in Eastern Europe and the Soviet Union were low endemic regions for HIV. It seemed as if the global HIV/AIDS epidemic had spared this geographical region".

Since then, the situation had changed radically. Luster writes, "With the collapse of the Soviet Union, a profound transformation took place in the structures in Eastern Europe and the former Soviet Union. Despite the heterogeneity [differences] of the regions, many similarities can be observed in all the countries concerned.

"Many countries have seen dramatic changes in their public health systems. Frequently, the level of staffing is insufficient or staffs are not paid. Investment and preventative measures are often inadequate or do not take place. Privatisation of the public health system has often led to two-tier health care, where part of the population [is] no longer adequately covered".

"Until the collapse of the Soviet Union, the countries in Eastern Europe and the Soviet Union were low endemic regions for HIV."

Hundreds of hospitals and other health facilities have been closed since the political changes of 1989–90, or have fallen into disrepair for lack of state funding. This process now continues apace as a result of the global economic crisis. In Latvia, for example, by the end of this year [2010], there will be just over one-third of the number of hospitals compared to 2009.

Throughout Eastern Europe, this social decline has now led to life expectancy shortening by seven years on average compared with 1989.

Health programmes and much-needed awareness campaigns do not exist or fall victim to the cutbacks. The report concludes that "the health systems in the 27 countries of the region have largely failed in the fight against HIV", and calls for a change in health and social policy in the fight against AIDS within the region.

But appeals to those in government fall on deaf ears. The governments of the region, which are often completely undemocratic and authoritarian regimes, are carrying through the destruction of previous social gains in consultation and collaboration with the International Monetary Fund (IMF) and the EU [European Union] in order to "attract investors".

Knowing full well that the pandemic can only be stopped by global access to medicines, improved health care and education, Western governments are cutting back on their spending for the fight against HIV/AIDS abroad.

While the costs for treatment rise, the funds that are made available are being decreased. According to the UN, funds made available by the G-8 nations [a group of eight wealthy countries] for the study of HIV in 2009 amounted to [US]$7.6 billion, less than the [US]$7.7 billion spent in 2008. Austria, for example, has completely cut its contribution to programmes combating HIV/AIDS abroad, on the grounds that government spending is too high.

In Asia, Discrimination Against Homosexual Men Hampers the Fight Against HIV/AIDS

Edmund Settle

Edmund Settle is the HIV/AIDS program specialist at the United Nations Development Programme (UNDP) in Beijing. In the following viewpoint, he notes that in the Asia Pacific region HIV/AIDS has particularly affected homosexual men. Because homosexuality is criminalized in many countries in the region, however, gay men have little access to health care to fight the disease. He concludes that legal reforms to protect gay men are needed if anti-AIDS efforts in the region are to be effective.

As you read, consider the following questions:

1. According to Settle, what problems do MSM (men who have sex with men) and transgender men face even in countries in areas where sex between men is not criminalized?

2. In what countries in the region does Settle say there have been recent laws and judicial or policy actions to protect the rights of MSM and transgender people?

3. Which four countries have specific strategic plans or action plans on MSM and HIV?

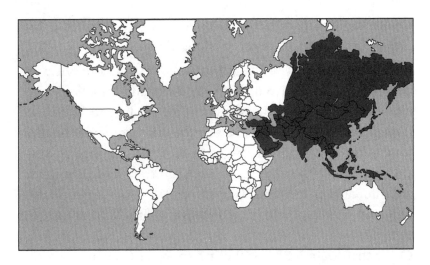

More than 90 percent of men having sex with men in the Asia Pacific region do not have access to HIV prevention and care services. HIV prevalence has reached alarming levels among men who have sex with men and transgender populations in many countries of Asia and the Pacific. If countries fail to address the legal context of the epidemic, this already critical situation is likely to become worse. The implementation of effective, human rights–based national HIV responses requires governments to consider the effect of laws and law enforcement practices on the health of men who have sex with men (MSM) and transgender persons.

Coinciding with the International Day Against Homophobia, this warning came as a key finding in the report on "Laws affecting HIV responses among men who have sex with men and transgender persons in Asia and the Pacific: an agenda for action". This forthcoming report with its key findings were reviewed today during the "High Level Dialogue on punitive laws, human rights and HIV prevention among men who have sex with men in the Asia Pacific Region" convened by the United Nations Development Programme (UNDP), the Asia Pacific Coalition on Male Sexual Health (APCOM) and the

Centre for Comparative and Public Law (CCPL) at the Faculty of Law, The University of Hong Kong.

The report showed that 19 of 48 countries in the Asia Pacific region criminalize male to male sex, and these laws often take on the force of vigilantism, often leading to abuse and human rights violations. Even in the absence of criminalization, other provisions of law often violate the rights of MSM and transgender persons along with arbitrary and inappropriate enforcement, thereby obstructing HIV interventions, advocacy and outreach, and service delivery. This very debate was at the heart of the recent landmark ruling by the Delhi High Court that Section 377 of the Indian Penal Code unfairly discriminates against men who have sex with men and consenting adults in general.

Furthermore, the report found that legislation and law enforcement often lag behind national HIV policies, with the result that the reach and effectiveness of programs for MSM and transgender persons are undermined. This indicates the need for greater coordination between health and justice sectors within government. There has been growing awareness among national policy makers of the need to identify MSM as a key population to be addressed by national HIV programmes.

The report showed that 19 of 48 countries in the Asia Pacific region criminalize male to male sex.

"The effectiveness of the HIV response will depend not just on the sustained scale-up of HIV prevention, treatment and care, but on whether the legal and social environments support or hinder programmes for those who are most vulnerable" said Mandeep Dhaliwal, UNDP Cluster Leader on Human Rights, Gender and Sexual Diversity. "The development and strengthening of an enabling legal and social environment is critical for comprehensive interventions for men who have sex with men and transgender people to have the greatest impact."

Finally, the study highlighted that there are some recent examples of protective laws, judicial and policy actions to improve the legal environment for MSM and transgender people, including important court judgments in Nepal, India, Pakistan, Philippines, Fiji, South Korea and Hong Kong. However, these are exceptional developments and action is required to improve the legal environment in all countries. Developing strategic partnerships and alliances between affected communities, the legal profession, human rights bodies, parliamentarians, and policy makers is critical.

The High Level Panelists, including former High Court Justices, and representatives from Parliament, civil society and the UN system, reviewed how comprehensive and rights-based HIV prevention among men who have sex with men and transgender people can occur only when a conducive and enabling legal environment is created. This will allow for unimpeded dissemination of prevention messages and services; appropriate provision of treatment, care and support services; and confidence-building measures among the most marginalized and vulnerable to seek essential information and access services.

"A strategy of comprehensive, rights-based HIV prevention requires bold and effective legal and policy measures to reach out to vulnerable communities and individuals at risk," stated the Honourable Michael Kirby of Australia. "It is here that reform of laws and law enforcement practices affecting private, adult same-sex activities must be seen as an imperative step in the path of reducing the isolation, stigma and vulnerability lived by communities and individuals. This will help enhance their self-respect and dignity as citizens and protect their legal rights, including receiving information on safer sex practices."

Many national HIV policies now accord a priority to MSM, even though the legal environment remains repressive. Some 22 national HIV responses in the Asia and Pacific region have identified MSM as a most-at-risk or priority population for the purposes of HIV prevention and four countries have specific strategic plans or action plans on MSM and HIV (Cambodia, China, Indonesia and India). Furthermore, a successful, community-led multi-country proposal to the Global Fund to Fight AIDS, Tuberculosis and Malaria on MSM and HIV has been endorsed by seven countries in South Asia.

"If society can display inclusiveness and understanding, MSM and transgender persons can be assured of a life of dignity and non-discrimination."

The Honorable Ajit Prakash Shah from India said, "If society can display inclusiveness and understanding, MSM and transgender persons can be assured of a life of dignity and non-discrimination. They cannot be excluded or ostracized merely because some of us perceive them as 'deviants' or 'different'. We should not forget that discrimination is the antithesis of equality and that it is the recognition of equality which will foster the dignity of every individual."

The preliminary findings reviewed at the High Level Dialogue are from a study commissioned by UNDP and APCOM. The study considered published research, legislation, legal cases and grey literature and drew from two regional consultations with community representatives and legal experts. The final report of the study's findings will be delivered at the XVIII International AIDS Conference, Vienna, at the session on Criminalizing Homosexual Behaviour: Human Rights Violation and Obstacles to Effective HIV/AIDS Prevention, 20 July 2010.

In Zambia, Discrimination Against Women Hampers the Fight Against HIV/AIDS

Nada Ali

Nada Ali is the Africa researcher for the Women's Rights Division of Human Rights Watch. In the following viewpoint, she reports that in Zambia, husbands are often able to beat or divorce their wives with impunity. In addition, HIV/AIDS is stigmatized. Because of these factors, Ali says, women fear revealing that they are HIV positive and frequently have trouble getting treatment. Ali concludes that to implement its HIV programs, Zambia needs to put in place stronger legal protections for women.

As you read, consider the following questions:

1. What does Ali say happened to the HIV-positive Ann after her husband divorced her?

2. What did the 1989 Intestate Succession Act do, according to Ali?

3. What does the author say must be done if Zambia's antiretroviral drug treatment (ART) program is to succeed?

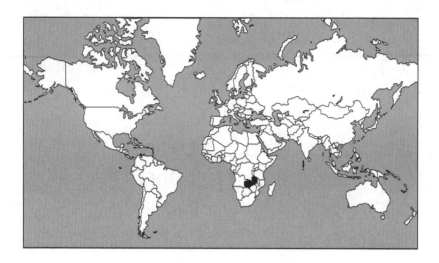

The Human Rights Council reviewed Zambia's report under its Universal Periodic Review (UPR) mechanism in Geneva last Friday (9 May), and adoption of the report took place this week on Wednesday (14 May). Here in Lusaka, women, including those who describe themselves as "living positively," are struggling to come out of the shadows that still obstruct the government's efforts to fight HIV/AIDS.

The premises of a women's support group in Lusaka are so obscure that every time I visited, the group's coordinator has had to meet me at a Zambeef shop on the main road before leading me through a labyrinth of muddy pathways that reminded me of some of the streets of Khartoum in my country, Sudan, in the morning after a rainy night. The voices and experiences of these women were strongly present when Human Rights Watch prepared its submission on Zambia for the UPR process.

Like dozens of other women that colleagues and I interviewed in Lusaka and the Copperbelt provinces, the support group members told me about their experiences with HIV and antiretroviral therapy (ART). A certain pattern started to unfold. Most of the women in the support group were either piece-workers or unemployed. They were all receiving HIV treatment, and nearly all of them were hiding their HIV status from their husbands or partners. The majority experienced excruciating physical, psychological or verbal abuse at the hands of their husbands, and this made it difficult for them to continue using the lifesaving treatment.

"I fear to tell my husband," said Maria (not her real name), a 45-year-old woman fearful of disclosing her HIV status at home. "He can shout and divorce me. He uses bad language with me." She told me that she hides her antiretroviral medicine. When she takes her pills, she said "I have to make sure that he is outside. That is why I forgot to take medicine."

They were all receiving HIV treatment, and nearly all of them were hiding their HIV status from their husbands or partners. The majority experienced excruciating physical, psychological, or verbal abuse at the hands of their husbands.

Maria's story is not unique. Nor are experiences of abuse limited to women who live in Lusaka. Women in Kafue, Chongwe, Ndola and Kitwe recounted similar ordeals that sometimes made them question their ability to start HIV treatment in the first place. When I interviewed Ann, a 27-year-old divorcee from Kafue, she had received an HIV-positive diagnosis on the previous day.

Ann was married according to customary law, and she said that upon divorcing her, her husband appropriated all her belongings, including plates, cupboards, mattresses and sheets. Ann said she complained to the headman of the farm where they lived, but her husband ran away to avoid confrontation with the headman. Ann said that she gave up trying to reclaim her badly needed belongings due to ill health.

Ann was due to return to the HIV clinic on the next day for further tests. Ann said that although the doctors might enroll her on ART, she might not be able to tolerate the medication without food. Unfortunately, the discrimination that Ann faces under customary law is sanctioned by Zambia's current constitution.

Although Zambia's rollout of free HIV treatment is commendable, and although more women than men are on HIV treatment in Zambia, the government has not done enough to ensure that women like Ann and Maria are able to start and, most importantly, continue using HIV treatment. Since drug resistance can occur and undermine treatment programs when patients are unable to adhere to their medications, there is very little scope for letting ART patients fail to take their drugs.

When asked whether health care workers and HIV treatment counselors discuss violence and other problems at home that might affect their treatment, the majority of the women told us that this only happened when they had visible bruises. Health care facilities providing ART have no systems in place to detect or address gender-based abuses such as domestic violence. The training that counselors receive does not cover violence against women in a systematic manner, nor does the understanding of gender-based abuses factor into official counselor certification.

Zambia has no specific law that criminalizes gender-based violence. The penal code does not cover marital rape or psychological abuse.

Zambia still lacks government protocols on how to deal with violence against women and other abuses within ART programs. And monitoring systems do not track the effects of such abuse. With the exception of the Coordinated Response Center for survivors of sexual and gender-based violence, our research found no partnerships in the health care system with institutions that could provide such services at health care facilities.

Similarly, the country's legal framework fails to address these issues adequately. Zambia has no specific law that criminalizes gender-based violence. The penal code does not cover marital rape or psychological abuse. Prevalent customary laws discriminate against women in terms of allocating property upon divorce or the death of a husband. Women's organizations told us that the 1989 Intestate Succession Act has led to a reduction in in-laws' grabbing widows' property, but it is ill-enforced. Addressing these legal shortcomings is important not only to protect women, but also essential for the success of Zambia's HIV-treatment programs.

It is true that Zambia has already made important steps toward introducing a gender-based violence bill, and has established the Victim Support Unit to address the needs of victims and survivors of gender-based violence. It is also true that Zambia's health system is already overstretched and severely understaffed. This will make it challenging to sustain programs that detect and respond to violence against women and other factors that obstruct women's HIV treatment. The majority of policy makers in the health sector and staff in health care facilities providing ART, however, told us that introducing initiatives that can respond to violence against women and other abuses would be feasible with sufficient guidelines, infrastructure, and staff training and support. Moreover, such initiatives should be carried out with support from the donor community and United Nations agencies.

Fortunately, there are already several guides produced by agencies such as the US Agency for International Development and the United Nations Population Fund that show how such programs could be integrated into health care facilities in countries with limited resources like Zambia. These initiatives range from providing information on violence against women and contact details for support groups, to having staff in clinics specifically trained to address violence against women.

AIDS in Zambia

Estimated adult HIV prevalence rate (aged 15–49), 2007	15.2
Estimated number of people (all ages) living with HIV, 2007 (thousands), estimate	1,100
Estimated number of people (all ages) living with HIV, 2007 (thousands), low estimate	1,000
Estimated number of people (all ages) living with HIV, 2007 (thousands), high estimate	1,200
Mother-to-child transmission, Estimated number of women (aged 15+) living with HIV, 2007 (thousands)	560
Paediatric infections, Estimated number of children (aged 0–14) living with HIV, 2007 (thousands)	95
Prevention among young people, HIV prevalence among young people (aged 15–24), 2007, male	3.6
Prevention among young people, HIV prevalence among young people (aged 15–24), 2007, female	11.3
Prevention among young people, % who have comprehensive knowledge of HIV, 2003–2008, male	37
Prevention among young people, % who have comprehensive knowledge of HIV, 2003–2008, female	34
Prevention among young people, % who used condom at last higher-risk sex, 2003–2008, male	48
Prevention among young people, % who used condom at last higher-risk sex, 2003–2008, female	38
Orphans, Children (aged 0–17) orphaned by AIDS, 2007, estimate (thousands)	600
Orphans, Children (aged 0–17) orphaned due to all causes, 2007, estimate (thousands)	1,100

TAKEN FROM: UNICEF, "Zambia: Statistics," March 2, 2010. http://www.unicef.org.

As an African woman working to promote women's rights in the continent, I was moved by the dignity and resilience of the Zambian women I interviewed. I was also impressed by these women's perseverance in high levels of adherence despite the abuse they face, and by the creative means they use to cope with indescribable adversity.

The government needs to introduce reforms in the health and legal systems to end the abuses against women that are obstructing their ability to fully benefit from lifesaving HIV-treatment programs.

Zambia's ART program is an impressive effort to provide free and universal HIV treatment. For this program to succeed, however, the government needs to introduce reforms in the health and legal systems to end the abuses against women that are obstructing their ability to fully benefit from lifesaving HIV-treatment programs.

The outcomes of Zambia's review, the final report of which will be adopted by the Human Rights Council in June 2008, can be seen as an expression of the consensus of the international community with regard to the human rights situation in Zambia. As such, Zambia's media and non-governmental organizations should take full advantage of the outcomes of the UPR, to press for legal and health-system reform in Zambia toward the elimination of abuses against women, including abuses that impede their HIV treatment.

In Indonesia, HIV/AIDS Intensifies Discrimination Against Women

Thaufiek Zulbahary, as told to Rochelle Jones

Rochelle Jones is a writer for the website of the Association for Women's Rights in Development (AWID); Thaufiek Zulbahary works with Solidaritas Perempuan, a women's rights organization in Indonesia. In the following viewpoint, Jones interviews Zulbahary about discrimination against women migrant workers in Indonesia. Zulbahary says that women—and especially female migrant workers—with HIV face increased discrimination and stigmatization. In addition, such women are often subject to sexual harassment, which may expose them to HIV. Zulbahary argues that women's rights groups need to focus on HIV/AIDS.

As you read, consider the following questions:

1. How does Solidaritas Perempuan campaign on issues of migration and trafficking, according to Zulbahary?

2. Through what methods does Zulbahary say that women with HIV find their right to work restricted in Indonesia?

3. What vulnerabilities to HIV/AIDS do female migrant workers face in the pre-departure phase, according to Zulbahary?

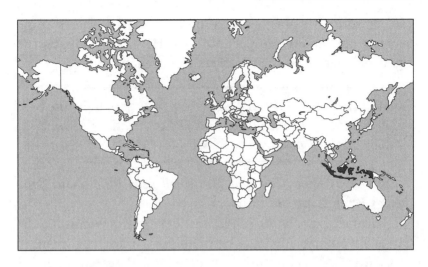

Arecent joint publication by BRIDGE and the International Community of Women Living with HIV and AIDS (ICW) highlights that "women and girls are especially vulnerable to HIV infection due to a host of biological, social, cultural and economic reasons, including women's entrenched social and economic inequality within sexual relationships and marriage. Globally there were 17.7 million women living with HIV in 2006—an increase of over one million compared with 2004. In sub-Saharan Africa, almost 60 percent of people living with HIV/AIDS in 2006 were women."

Gender Inequality and HIV/AIDS

There is a two-way relationship between entrenched gender inequality and HIV/AIDS, however. Whilst it is well known that women are more vulnerable to HIV infection because of intersectional inequality within society, women living with HIV/AIDS are further marginalised and suffer from inequality and rights violations because they are HIV positive.

So how does HIV/AIDS impact on women's rights and what do some women's rights organisations focus on for more effective and gender-sensitive responses to HIV/AIDS? Thaufiek Zulbahary, who works for Solidaritas Perempuan

(SP), a women's rights organisation in Indonesia, shared some valuable and unique insight into how HIV/AIDS impacts the rights of migrant women workers in Indonesia.

Women living with HIV/AIDS are further marginalised and suffer from inequality and rights violations because they are HIV positive.

Rochelle Jones: *Can you please tell us a little about Solidaritas Perempuan and the work that you do?*

Thaufiek Zulbahary: Solidaritas Perempuan/Women's Solidarity for Human Rights is based in Jakarta and is a member of CARAM Asia (Coordination of Action Research on AIDS and Mobility in Asia) and the Asia Pacific Forum on Women, Law and Development (APWLD). SP's programs related to migration, trafficking and HIV/AIDS are:

1. Policy Advocacy. This includes monitoring and analysing policies regarding migration and trafficking, migration and health (HIV/AIDS). We also conduct advocacy research, such as research on the vulnerability of migrants to HIV/AIDS; the state of health of Indonesian migrant workers (access to health), and research on the mandatory testing of migrant workers. We also respond to actual political economic situations through lobbying decision makers and we focus on strengthening and building alliances with other organisations to encourage policy change.

2. Migrant Workers' Empowerment Against HIV/AIDS. This program aims to empower migrant workers, families and grassroots organisations in their source area about HIV/AIDS and migration issues. Migrant workers and their families are involved in some research to map out and build strategies to counter their problems with HIV/AIDS. In addition we provide and disseminate information services for migrant workers related to HIV/AIDS and trafficking.

3. Legal Aid. Providing legal aid and assistance related with referral services for women migrant workers with HIV/AIDS and those who become victims of trafficking.

4. Campaigning. We are regularly campaigning on issues of migration and trafficking, and migration and health (HIV/AIDS) through press conferences, talk shows on TV and radio, discussions, book reviews, public dialogue, etc. SP also produces campaign materials such as brochures, stickers, pins, fact sheets, clothes and posters and SP's bulletin.

Women Migrant Workers and HIV/AIDS

How does HIV/AIDS impact women's rights?

Based on SP's experience establishing a program of HIV/AIDS for women migrant workers, we have identified numerous impacts of HIV/AIDS on women's rights.

Women migrant workers suffer various kinds of injustices as a result of being infected with HIV/AIDS, one of which is the violation of their right to work. For example, migrant workers in Indonesia, 70% of which are women, are obliged to have a medical test (including HIV test) before their departure to foreign countries and then when they arrive on work sites. Unfit migrant workers, especially those who suffer from HIV/AIDS, are not allowed to work abroad. If by the time they have another medical check in receiving countries they are discovered to be infected with HIV, they are sent home/deported.

Women with HIV/AIDS experience more discrimination and stigmatisation because of their health status. This comes from family, society, institutions (including hospitals) and the government. For example: With HIV, women will soon be labeled as promiscuous or as prostitutes or disobedient to religious values. Women with HIV are often forced to hide their health status based on the desire of the family because the disease is considered shameful, so only mothers are allowed to know. The rest of the family only know that the woman is suffering a serious illness (for example: TB). In hospital, many nurses and paramedics are hesitant and afraid of giving treatment, they often move the patient around as a gesture of avoidance. Patients with HIV/AIDS are often placed in the same location as patients with other diseases, again, such as TB.

Women are often considered as the spreading agent of HIV/AIDS. On one side, the campaign to use female condoms can be seen as contributing to the assumption of women being the problem source and at the same time it adds to women's burden in preventing HIV/AIDS.

Women with HIV/AIDS experience more discrimination and stigmatisation because of their health status. This comes from family, society, institutions (including hospitals) and the government.

HIV/AIDS is also related to women's reproductive health and children's growth. Mothers with HIV/AIDS who are pregnant are advised to have a caesarean birth to prevent their child from HIV infection. Furthermore, they are told they can't breast-feed their child and breast milk is replaced with formula milk for the baby. This influences their emotional relationship with their child and the growth of the baby (physically and mentally).

Sexual Harassment and HIV

Why should women's rights organizations be focusing on HIV/ AIDS?

Based on SP's research about the unique vulnerability of migrant workers (MWs) to AIDS in 2004, 2005, and 2006, we found that MWs are vulnerable to HIV/AIDS in every stage of migration (pre-departure, post-arrival, and reintegration). Specific vulnerabilities to HIV/AIDS during the migration process include:

The Plight of Indonesian Migrant Workers

Since the 1970s, tens of millions of Indonesians have left the country to work as maids, nannies, drivers and laborers in hope of a better life.

Some make it. But many do not, returning home with no money, beaten, depressed or, at worst, in a coffin. As many as 60 percent of Indonesians who travel overseas to work face serious problems, ranging from physical abuse to not being paid and as far as being killed on the job or committing suicide out of despair. Ministry of Foreign Affairs records show that on average a shocking six Indonesian migrants die daily—mostly migrant workers.

Dewi Kurniawati and Hera Diani;
"The Misery of Indonesia's Migrant Workers,"
JakartaGlobe, *August 19, 2009. http://thejakartaglobe.com.*

Pre-Departure Phase. During the recruitment process sexual harassment and rape can be perpetuated by the Broker ('Calo'). At the medical check, prospective women MWs only wear underwear as they undergo their medical check, which makes them vulnerable to sexual abuse. In addition, there is a lack of information among the potential MWs that HIV/AIDS can be transmitted by infected needles. Most MWs do not have the confidence while they are in the hospital to ask for a sterile needle. In the Holding Centre, sexual harassment or rape by holding centre personnel may take place, as well as sexual relations (be it voluntary or forced).

Post Arrival (On-Site). The main factors causing vulnerability are sexual relations (be it voluntary or forced) and the quality of medical checks and health services in destination countries. Other factors of vulnerability on-site include loneliness, homesickness and social isolation, economic pressure, harsh working and living conditions, a lack of access to health services and information and gender injustices faced by migrant workers. Women are mostly placed in vulnerable workplaces, such as domestic and entertainment workers, which makes them vulnerable to sexual harassment and abuse by their employer, [colleagues], and customers.

Returning Home (Reintegration). Women experience sexual harassment and rape, perpetuated by airport personnel and taxi drivers at and from the airport, sexual relations (be it voluntary or forced).

Women are mostly placed in vulnerable workplaces, such as domestic and entertainment workers, which makes them vulnerable to sexual harassment and abuse by their employer, [colleagues], and customers.

Women whose spouses are MWs are vulnerable to HIV/AIDS because biologically, women are more 'easily' infected and there is limited information on HIV/AIDS and migration realities. Women trust their husbands' fidelity; are economically more dependent than their male partners; have lesser or no negotiating power for safer sex; and have lesser or no access to information and services on HIV/AIDS. Violence against women also makes women more vulnerable to HIV/AIDS.

Generally, factors of women MWs' vulnerability to HIV/AIDS are: The feminisation of migration (most of Indonesia's MWs are women); lack of information on HIV/AIDS and migration realities; inadequate programs to inform migrant workers on HIV/AIDS; too many people in each orientation class, wrong information, limited time, and top-down method (pre-departure orientation seminar (PDOS) and Pre-Departure Training); difficulties in reaching out to excluded people (e.g.

domestic worker); mandatory HIV antibody testing in Indonesia and destination countries; low rate of condom use and poor health-seeking behaviour.

Thus, the role of women's organisations (including our organisation) is vital in order to empower and give the appropriate information to women about HIV/AIDS, their rights (e.g. rights to health, rights to work) along with efforts in advocating for the just regulation on stipulating prevention acts toward HIV/AIDS.

Periodical and Internet Sources Bibliography

The following articles have been selected to supplement the diverse views presented in this chapter.

AIDS-Free World	"Jamaican Prime Minister Supports Outdated Laws," March 6, 2009. www.aidsfreeworld.org.
Tifa Asrianti	"Women with HIV Face Greater Risks," *Jakarta Post*, November 30, 2010.
AVERT	"HIV & AIDS Stigma and Discrimination." www.avert.org.
Jason Beaubien	"Mexico Tackles AIDS Discrimination," *NPR*, August 8, 2008.
Child Rights Information Network	"Editorial: Children's Rights and HIV and AIDS," December 1, 2010. www.crin.org.
Angella Musiimenta	"Stigma and Discrimination Surrounding HIV/ AIDS," Women Deliver, August 18, 2010. www.womendeliver.org.
Laura Nyblade et al.	"Disentangling HIV and AIDS Stigma in Ethiopia, Tanzania and Zambia," International Center for Research on Women, 2003. www.icrw.org.
Peter O'Neil	"Stigma Hurts Senegal's AIDS Battle," *Edmonton Journal*, January 6, 2010.
Madhulika Sonkar	"HIV Positive Children Battle Disease, Discrimination," *Headlines India*, December 1, 2010.
VOANews.com	"Study Links Discrimination of Homosexuals with Rising HIV Cases in Asia," July 21, 2010. www.voanews.com.

For Further Discussion

Chapter 1

1. Based on the viewpoints by Alex Blaze and Michael Fitzpatrick, do you think it is accurate to say that there is currently an AIDS crisis in the West? Is it best to err on the side of saying there is a crisis even if there may not be one? Explain your reasoning.

2. If AIDS had begun in the United States, would it have an AIDS epidemic like the one in Africa? Base your argument on the viewpoints by John Iliffe and Noel Dzimnenani Mbirimtengerenji.

3. Some religious leaders have argued that condom use worsens AIDS epidemics, because it encourages promiscuity and damages traditional morality. Do the experiences of Senegal and the Philippines support this position? In your answer, consider the articles by the United States Agency for International Development and Eugenio M. Caccam Jr.

Chapter 2

1. Rupa Chinai argues that poor nutrition contributes to AIDS. Do all people with AIDS suffer from poor nutrition? Does this undermine Chinai's argument? Explain your reasoning.

2. Based on all the viewpoints in this section, is the treatment of AIDS solely a scientific question, or does it raise moral issues as well? Explain your answer.

Chapter 3

1. How do the cases discussed by Rosie DiManno and Gisela Friedrichsen differ, and do you believe that the outcomes in these cases were fair? Explain your answer.

2. Based on the viewpoints by Karl Vick, Jarrett Zigon, Timothy Finigan, and Ben Goldacre, does it seem like it is more acceptable to distribute free needles for drug addicts than to distribute condoms? Should the moral choices differ for needles and condoms? Explain your answer.

Chapter 4

1. In Chapter 3, Jarrett Zigon notes that many in the Russian Orthodox Church believe that the spread of AIDS in Eastern Europe is the result of moral breakdown. Does Markus Salzmann agree with this analysis? Do Nina Ferencic, Ruslan Malyuta, Paul Nary, and Jadranka Mimica? Explain your answer.

2. Based on the viewpoints in this chapter, does discrimination against AIDS victims hurt only those discriminated against, or does it harm those who discriminate as well? Explain your answer.

Organizations to Contact

The editors have compiled the following list of organizations concerned with the issues debated in this book. The descriptions are derived from materials provided by the organizations. All have publications or information available for interested readers. The list was compiled on the date of publication of the present volume; the information provided here may change. Be aware that many organizations take several weeks or longer to respond to inquiries, so allow as much time as possible.

Amnesty International USA

5 Penn Plaza, New York, NY   10001

(212) 807-8400 • fax: (212) 627-1451

e-mail: aimember@aiusa.org

website: www.amnestyusa.org

Amnesty International is a worldwide movement of people who campaign for internationally recognized human rights. Its vision is of a world in which every person enjoys all of the human rights enshrined in the Universal Declaration of Human Rights and other international human rights standards. Each year it publishes a report on its work and its concerns throughout the world. Amnesty International highlights the connection between human rights and HIV/AIDS prevention through, for example, its website page "A Human Rights Approach to HIV/AIDS." It also publishes numerous individual country reports and briefings, such as "Love, Hate, and the Law: Decriminalizing Homosexuality."

AVERT

4 Brighton Road, Horsham, West Sussex   RH13 5BA
   United Kingdom

+44 (0)1403 210202

e-mail: info@avert.org

website: www.avert.org

The international HIV and AIDS charity AVERT works to reduce the number and impact of infections globally through education and promotion of positive, proactive treatment of the disease. Many of the organization's projects focus on Africa and India, with an emphasis on prevention as well as aid for those already affected by AIDS. AVERT's website offers regional summaries of the AIDS epidemic as well as more detailed, specific reports about the prevalence of the disease within particular countries such as South Africa, Malawi, and Uganda. The website also offers resources targeted at gay men and women, such as the booklet *Young Gay Men Talking.*

Caritas Internationalis

Palazzo San Calisto, Vatican City State   V-00120
+ 39 06 698 797 99 • fax: + 39 06 698 872 37
e-mail: caritas.internationalis@caritas.va
website: www.caritas.org

Caritas Internationalis is a confederation of Roman Catholic relief, development, and social service organizations. Its mission is to build a better world, especially for the poor and oppressed. Caritas is involved in disaster relief, sustainable development, and peace building. Its website includes news, bulletins, and access to the organization's annual report. A section of the website is devoted to the topic "How Caritas Works: HIV and AIDS."

Global AIDS Alliance Fund

1121 Fourteenth Street NW, Suite 200
Washington, DC   20005
(202) 789-0432 • fax: (202) 789-0715
e-mail: info@globalaidsalliancefund.org
website: www.globalaidsalliancefund.org

The Global AIDS Alliance Fund was founded to help accelerate an end to global HIV/AIDS and extreme poverty. The organization conducts public education and media outreach to raise awareness and engages in citizen-based advocacy and lobbying to hold government leaders accountable for concrete action. The Global AIDS Alliance Fund publishes numerous fact sheets, such as "Global AIDS Statistics."

Human Rights Watch

350 Fifth Avenue, 34th Floor, New York, NY   10118-3299
(212) 290-4700 • fax: (212) 736-1300
e-mail: hrwnyc@hrw.org
website: www.hrw.org

Founded in 1978, Human Rights Watch conducts systematic investigations of human rights abuses in countries around the world. The nongovernmental organization opposes discrimination against those with HIV/AIDS. It publishes many books and reports on specific countries and issues as well as annual reports and other articles, such as "Comments to Uganda's Parliamentary Committee on HIV/AIDS and Related Matters about the HIV/AIDS Prevention and Control Bill."

UK Consortium on AIDS and International Development

Grayston Centre, 28 Charles Square, London   N1 6HT
   United Kingdom
44 (0)20-7324-4780
e-mail: info@aidsconsortium.org.uk
website: www.aidsconsortium.org.uk

The UK Consortium on AIDS and International Development works to encourage, initiate, and support collaborative action by civil society to contribute to and influence the global response to HIV and AIDS. The Stop AIDS Campaign is an initiative of the UK Consortium on AIDS and International Development, bringing together more than eighty of the United Kingdom's leading development and HIV and AIDS groups to raise awareness in the United Kingdom about the global HIV/AIDS epidemic. The consortium publishes a number of policy briefings and reports, such as "HIV and Health Systems Strengthening: Opportunities for Achieving Universal Access by 2010."

UNAIDS

UNAIDS Secretariat, 20, Avenue Appia, Geneva 27   CH-1211
   Switzerland
+41.22.791.3666 • fax: +41.22.791.4187
e-mail: aidsinfo@unaids.org
website: www.unaids.org

UNAIDS, the Joint United Nations Programme on HIV/AIDS,
is the United Nations' agency providing efforts to internationally combat the AIDS epidemic. The organization focuses its
efforts on areas such as prevention, treatment, and care; populations most affected by the disease; the broader effects of the
disease on communities; and general research into vaccines
and preventive measures. UNAIDS has published numerous
documents detailing all aspects of this global disease, with
most reports available on the organization's website in por-
table document format (pdf).

United Nations Children's Fund (UNICEF)

3 United Nations Plaza, New York, NY   10017
(212) 326-7000 • fax: (212) 887-7465
website: www.unicef.org

The United Nations Children's Fund (UNICEF) works to help
build a world where the rights of every child are realized. The
organization works to prevent the spread of HIV among young
people and helps children and families affected by HIV/AIDS
to live with dignity. UNICEF publishes numerous briefing papers, available at its website, such as "Scaling up Early Infant
Diagnosis and Linkages to Care and Treatment."

William J. Clinton Foundation

55 West 125th Street, New York, NY   10027
(212) 348-8882
website: www.clintonfoundation.org

The William J. Clinton Foundation focuses on worldwide issues that demand urgent action, solutions, and measurable results. The Clinton HIV/AIDS Initiative (CHAI) works to ne-

gotiate lower prices for lifesaving antiretroviral drug treatment in the developing world and works with governments to improve the national health care systems required to deliver crucial medicines. The William J. Clinton Foundation publishes information about CHAI, including reports about its access programs.

World Bank
1818 H Street NW, Washington, DC 20433
(202) 473-1000 • fax: (202) 477-6391
website: www.worldbank.org

The World Bank is a source of financial and technical assistance for developing countries around the world. The World Bank provides low-interest loans, interest-free credits, and grants to developing countries for a wide array of purposes such as investments in health, public administration, and infrastructure. Among the World Bank's publications are the reports *The Africa Multi-Country AIDS Program 2000–2006* and *The World Bank's Commitment to HIV/AIDS in Africa: Our Agenda for Action 2007–2011.*

Bibliography of Books

Tony Barnett and Alan Whiteside
AIDS in the Twenty-First Century, Fully Revised and Updated Edition: Disease and Globalization. New York: Palgrave Macmillan, 2002.

James Chin
The AIDS Pandemic: The Collision of Epidemiology with Political Correctness. Oxon, UK: Radcliffe Publishing, 2007.

Hansjörg Dilger and Ute Luig, eds.
Morality, Hope and Grief: Anthropologies of AIDS in Africa. New York: Berghahn Books, 2010.

Timothy Edgar, Seth M. Noar, and Vicki S. Freimuth, eds.
Communication Perspectives on HIV/ AIDS for the 21st Century. New York: Lawrence Erlbaum Associates, 2008.

Jonathan Engel
The Epidemic: A Global History of AIDS. New York: Smithsonian Books/ Collins, 2006.

Helen Epstein
The Invisible Cure: Why We Are Losing the Fight Against AIDS in Africa. New York: Picador, 2008.

Andrew Holleran
Chronicle of a Plague, Revisited: AIDS and Its Aftermath. New York: Da Capo Press, 2008.

Susan S. Hunter
AIDS in America. New York: Palgrave Macmillan, 2006.

Susan S. Hunter
AIDS in Asia: A Continent in Peril. New York: Palgrave Macmillan, 2005.

Mary Jo Iozzio, ed.   *Calling for Justice Throughout the World: Catholic Women Theologians on the HIV/AIDS Pandemic.* New York: Continuum, 2008.

Seth C. Kalichman   *Denying AIDS: Conspiracy Theories, Pseudoscience, and Human Tragedy.* New York: Copernicus, 2009.

S.S. Abdool Karim and Q. Abdool Karim, eds.   *HIV/AIDS in South Africa.* New York: Cambridge University Press, 2008.

James F. Keenan   *Catholic Ethicists on HIV/AIDS Prevention.* New York: Continuum, 2000.

Shao-hau Liu   *Passage to Manhood: Youth Migration, Heroin, and AIDS in Southwest China.* Stanford, CA: Stanford University Press, 2011.

Stephen Moses et al.   *AIDS in South Asia: Understanding and Responding to a Heterogeneous Epidemic.* Washington, DC: World Bank, 2006.

Mead Over et al.   *HIV/AIDS Treatment and Preventions in India: Modeling the Cost and Consequences.* Washington, DC: World Bank, 2004.

Kenneth R. Overberg   *Ethics and AIDS: Compassion and Justice in Global Crisis.* Lanham, MD: Rowman & Littlefield Publishers, Inc., 2006.

Elizabeth Pisani	*The Wisdom of Whores: Bureaucrats, Brothels and the Business of AIDS.* New York: W.W. Norton & Company, 2008.
Vasu Reddy, Theo Sandfort, and Laetitia Rispel, eds.	*From Social Silence to Social Science: Same-Sex Sexuality, HIV & AIDS and Gender in South Africa.* Cape Town, South Africa: HSRC Press, 2009.
Jarrett Zigon	*HIV Is God's Blessing: Rehabilitating Morality in Neoliberal Russia.* Berkeley: University of California Press, 2010.

Index

Geographic headings and page numbers in **boldface** refer to viewpoints about that country or region.